*Listening in a Loud World*

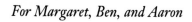
*For Margaret, Ben, and Aaron*

*Listening in a Loud World*

*Toward a Theology of Meaning*

Robert C. Shippey, Jr.

Mercer University Press
Macon, Georgia

© 2005 Mercer University Press
1400 Coleman Avenue
Macon, Georgia 31207
All rights reserved
MUP/P300
First Edition.

Permission to use images of Picasso's works courtesy of
©Estate of Pablo Picasso/Artists Rights Society (ARS),
New York and for all images Art Resource, 536 Broadway,
New York NY 10012

*Library of Congress Cataloging-in-Publication Data*

Shippey, Robert C.
Listening in a loud world : toward a theology of
meaning / Robert C.
Shippey, Jr.-- 1st edition.
p. cm.
Includes bibliographical references and index.
ISBN-13: 978-0-86554-951-7 (pbk. : alk. paper)
ISBN-10: 0-86554-951-6 (pbk. : alk. paper)
1. Listening—Religious aspects—Christianity.
2. Christian life. I.
Title.
BV4647.L56.S35 2005
248.4—dc22
2005020725

# Contents

# Listening

What is the voice that speaks in subtle tone?
What lesson is there in the tremor and the groan?

Where is God?
Where are we?
Where is the church,
and do the righteous flee?

The Divine is in the wind's call,
and God is in the silence.
But we are in the busy labor
struggling with the consequence.

God's love is
holy radiance,
and we but need to listen
to transforming recompense.

How does grace draw near,
and for whom does love encompass?
Divine presence gives life
in the hurt and humus.

Creator and rest
in Whom we begin,
Grace reaching, rippling, near forever
carrying us to destiny's end.

(continued)

Light unto darkness
is the journey's way.
Darkness unto light
is silence's sway.

We move from faith to meaning
in love's pure melody.
We listen to redemption's transfusion,
that subtly sets us free.

# Acknowledgments

Listening that discerns the Holy begins with a steadfast commitment never to sell the soul's birthright for a bowl of pottage. Jacob and Esau teach us this much, yet sadly, too many people rely too heavily on others to lead them and give them the right view of truth with little appreciation for the right search for truth to which each of us has been called. Imperative for real faith is an intentional commitment to listen to the call of God that always seeks to transform us. Like Abraham of old, each of us has been called to leave the familiar in search of a new, far more enriching land. The only question is: will we have the courage to listen and the will to follow God to the places where God gently invites us?

I arrived at Shorter College in January 2003 to find myself embarking on a new chapter in my professional life. The learning environment at Shorter College readily impressed me, as its focus was on the uncompromising search for truth—wherever it might lead. For me, listening to the call of wisdom and trusting its process is what makes an authentic community of learning. Faith here was understood as the ability to make sense of one's life, and the search for genuine relationships with each other and with God was honored. I discovered a trust between faculty, students, and the administration that allowed for a free exchange of ideas void of intimidation and narrow-mindedness.

Interesting though was the challenge of writing at a time where the institution was involved in litigation with the Georgia Baptist Convention concerning institutional ownership and authority to appoint governing trustees. Disconcerting uncertainty was most often the norm, but the waiting also reminded me to listen always for the grace of God. The Georgia Supreme Court, in a 4-3 ruling, determined eventually that the college could not divest itself of the Georgia Baptist Convention. Only time will tell the extent to which this ruling will affect the learning environment as well as spiritual context for authentic discernment of meaning at this beloved institution.

I will always be grateful to President Ed Schrader and Provost Harold Newman for extending an invitation to become a part of Shorter College. In doing so, I was provided an opportunity to pause and ponder how once listens to the presence of God in the chaotic confusion of our world.

Holy listening and the quandary as to why good people in the Christian faith so often talk past each other is indicative of the rampant spiritual confusion of postmodernity. I am a product of Baptists who have fought with each other the last twenty-five years. In the theological preoccupation with their own self-interests, they have been too busy squabbling to take time to focus on the interests of others in need of a great portion of God's love. Baptists are perhaps the worst example, but they are not alone, as other mainline denominations have struggled as well for identity and absolute clarity in a relativistic world.

In such a contentious and changing context, I have sought to discover anew what it means to listen to God. I am grateful for the many students, laypersons, teachers, and clergy who have provided a forum in which to think aloud about the importance of holy listening. While these people are not mentioned by name, they have provided countless insights through their reflections and faith.

In his role as dean, Rob Nash has provided encouragement, and his insights have been helpful throughout the development of the book. More importantly, he has been my friend for more than half the years I have inhabited this earth, and I am blessed to journey with him in our efforts to listen to God. I also want to thank Laura McRaney, the administrative assistant for the School of Religion and International Studies, who labored through the manuscript and made many helpful suggestions in its development. Kim Herndon and the Shorter College Livingston Library staff are thanked for all of their help in securing many needed resources. Finally, I want to extend a word of heartfelt appreciation to my editors at Mercer University Press, Marc Jolley and Kevin Manus. I remain grateful for their enthusiasm for the book and willingness to publish it.

My father died in the early stages of writing, and I regret that he did not live long enough to see this work materialize. He and my mother sacrificed much to give me the education and opportunities that have come my way. They are the reason that I am a child of the church, and the faith they bequeathed has sustained me on my journey toward God. My wife, Cheryl, has listened to countless versions of this book and has been helpful in so many ways. Her ongoing joke has been that she would write the last line, knowing much better than I will ever admit how far I still have to go in the journey toward listening. Finally, as my parents gave faith to me, this book is dedicated to and written mostly for my children— Margaret, Ben and Aaron—who provide countless moments of joy and insight about the end to which listening always points, which is God's love. My greatest hope is that this gift will encourage them in their own journeys toward meaning.

Robert Shippey
The Hill
23 May 2005

# List of Illustrations

# 1

# *Introduction*

We learn to listen before we learn to speak, read, or write. Listening is the basic building block of communication. The degree to which we can listen is the degree to which we can understand, and the degree to which we can understand is the measure by which we enjoy living. But listening is not easy.

Constant messages come our way. Cell phones, e-mail, pagers, faxes, internet, radio, and television overwhelm our auditory senses and constantly invade our space. Through these mediums, we are told what we must have in order to be whole, and we are made to feel less than adequate if we do not possess whatever it is that materialism is promising. Such inadequacy can result in feelings of emptiness that make it difficult to hear. Our world too is much more vulnerable, and we find ourselves more aware than ever of the reality of life's finitude. It is hard to listen when the pain is intense, the hurt is real, and the fear is heightened! In addition, some people have a difficult time physically hearing and can easily become frustrated. They may tire of making the effort to hear. By choice, if not by consequence, they find themselves moving more deeply into a lonely world of isolation. But in a loud world where both external and internal factors make it difficult to hear each other let alone the presence of the divine, the need for listening is acute.

## The Need for Holy Listening

Intentional listening or, as I like to refer to it, holy listening is necessary because of the hectic pace most of us are required to maintain. The burden of moving at neck-breaking speed does not easily allow for openness to God, the need of others, and the desire for a fulfilled sense of self. There are many more than willing to tell us how to experience God and how to establish a purpose for living, but too few willing to speak about the need for trust and the need to journey into the depth of our souls to discover something new about ourselves, our neighbors, and God. We need to do more than just hear simplistic answers that pale in comparison to our complex world, and faith needs to be more than just a wave of emotion interpreted through the lenses of our need to be entertained in worship. Holy listening requires the use of the heart, mind, ears, and eyes. Where we do so, there is the possibility of engaging meaning at a spiritual depth necessary to open our lives to the fullness of God, the vitality of community, and the calling of humble service. The intent of this book is to help the reader develop a faith that seeks understanding and makes real meaning in a world of chatter.

Because holy listening entails use of the heart, mind, ears, and eyes, this book includes a focal painting in each chapter. I cannot help but wonder if the real prophets are the painters and the poets whose message calls forth in bold ways the need to move beyond simple faith to a depth of spiritual awareness that recognizes the presence of the living God in every moment of our lives. Those who want to hear the prophet's message in the vivid colors and stark contrast of light will do well to examine the paintings from as many different angles as possible in order to discern the depth of meaning conveyed. Similarly, the book addresses numerous biblical passages and their relevance for holy listening. Just as the various paintings can be observed from different perspectives, the discerning listener will also want to consider the nuances of scripture and the levels of meaning contained within. By doing so, the reader gains the opportunity to listen to the fullness of God's Word and its claim on our lives, instead of insisting that this Word be received through the predetermined biases and claims we bring to the text.

Exploring why listening is so difficult and examining key hermeneutical issues related to scripture, the nature of God, the journey of faith, and our own human limits are addressed. The book also examines the spiritual need for holy listening and analyzes critical questions of faith that lead to a greater awareness of self and the church in the mutual calling to be the incarnation of Jesus Christ in a postmodern world. Essential in holy listening is an awareness of the theological importance of rest and the role the Sabbath plays in providing an opportunity to embrace the redemptive work of God. Also emphasized is the need for both faith as a linear journey toward wholeness and faith as an ability to make home and community along life's way. The place of hope in the midst of suffering and the need to listen for joy in the face of pain are also explored, even at a personal level where I seek to listen for the presence of God in my daughter's struggle with the chronic illness of diabetes. The book will conclude by discussing the spiritual value of silence as the way to experience anew the redemptive story of Jesus who beckons us to a life of service and love.

## Components of Holy Listening

The idea for this book was born out of my own physically diminished capacity to hear. Chronic ear trouble has been both a bane and a blessing. Even in the midst of intense pain induced by the inflammation of the inner ear, I have learned to listen to the only voice that can comfort on the other side of pain which is the voice of God's love. Finding peace in an isolated world where only the sufferer can sojourn awakened me at an early age to the gift of silence that opens one to his or her center. Knowing or experiencing such centeredness is difficult to explain, but I am reminded of a time in my youth when I was in Brigadoon—kilt and all! A dance instructor was brought in to teach the actors how to dance. I had a difficult time spinning my body around without becoming dizzy until the instructor taught me to fix my eyes on one point and to look at that point every time I turned around. Having this "north star" to focus on kept me from losing my balance. Similarly, the intensity of pain can force one to focus on the center of his or her existence in a way that gives both clarity and solace.

The difficulty in hearing has also taught me to listen not just with my ears, but also by observing facial expressions, hand gestures, eye contact, and body movement. Try listening with your eyes sometime. Even more importantly, try listening with your heart. Holy listening can render a greater awareness of the presence of God than what casual prayer and routine worship offer, but such holy listening begins in silence with a still heart and mind.

The reality is that listening and hearing are not the same. Genuine listening is the ability to convert the sounds that impact the eardrums into real meaning of the mind and the heart. Language itself is but a symbol of a deeper meaning to which we are drawn and have a desire to comprehend. Adler, Rosenfeld, and Towne define listening as involving five separate elements that include "hearing, attending, understanding, remembering and responding."[1] They define hearing as a physiological process that involves sound waves impacting the eardrum. Attending is the second component, which is the means by which we filter out some messages and receive others based on our needs and based on our comfort, trust, and confidence in the one giving us information. In other words, we are more inclined to listen when we trust the message and see the benefits. Understanding is the third component, which deals with the ability of the listener to interpret, critically reflect, and discern the meaning of the message that is conveyed. The fourth factor is the process of remembering that includes recall and selection of information and knowledge that we want to maintain. Recall is difficult. Just think about how hard it is to remember someone's name let alone the content of what they are sharing. Adler cites research that details that we remember only about half of what we immediately hear. After eight hours, we only retain about 35 percent of the message and after two months, we retain only about a quarter of the original information.[2] Adler goes

---

[1] Ronal B. Adler, Lawrence B. Rosenfeld, and Neil Towne, *Interplay: The Process of Interpersonal Communication* (Fort Worth: Harcourt Brace College Publishers, 1995) 114. See also 114–17.

[2] Ibid., 116.

on to observe that "the more intensity, intimacy, trust and commitment in the relationship, the more we pay attention to what others are saying."[3] The final aspect of listening involves responding to the information or message. Responding includes non-verbal responses like eye contact and facial expressions as well as verbal responses that include answering questions and exchanging ideas and knowledge. The authors conclude their definition of listening by quoting Norman R. Augustine who says, "One often hears the remark, 'He talks too much,' but when did anyone last hear the criticism 'He listens too much'?"[4]

One could say the same of prayer. We might criticize someone for praying too long, but when was the last time someone was criticized for listening too much in the time of prayer? Holy listening is the process by which we take all of the messages we receive and assess them in light of what we sense our soul calling us to be. Hearing, attending, understanding, remembering, and responding are all vital components of authentic prayer and intentional listening to the Spirit of God. This book is about rediscovering the process regarding how we become more aware of the presence of divine love in order to discern more clearly our calling, meaning, purpose, and desire to lean toward God.

The ancient Hebrew refused to separate the body from the soul and the spirit from the mind. For them, the body was a psychosomatic whole that represented the perfect blend of body, mind, and emotions. They could not conceive of separating these characteristics, because each was necessary to sustain the life of the other. What they also realized was that the lifelong quest for meaning included the elevation of all that is material into the spiritual realm. The need was to understand the pervasive presence of God in all that is and to incorporate all that we are and have into this divine mystery.

Consistent with the Hebraic way of thinking, holy listening requires engagement of our whole being. To hear God is to

---

[3] Ibid., 116–17.
[4] Ibid., 117.

experience the divine with our body, mind, emotions, and soul. If the deep is to draw into the deep, it cannot be at a level where only the emotions are stirred. Equally, holy listening requires more than just a mental affirmation that God exists. An encounter with the divine requires an openness to think in new and imaginative ways about God and a willingness to confess our limitations of divine knowledge in light of human finitude. Moreover, for the Christian, all that is material, including thoughts and possessions, must give way to a love for Jesus that exceeds a love of selfish interests, including commitments to the church, the denomination, a particular version or translation of the Bible, and a particular niche on the market of truth.

The Chinese characters that make up the verb "to listen" remind us of the significant skill required in listening through the combined linking of characters for ear, eyes, undivided attention, and heart.[5] The symbol is akin to Jesus' call in the gospel to love the Lord our God with all our heart, mind, strength, and soul (Mark 12:28–32). Listening to the transcendent with this kind of passion enables us to experience the promised land of God's presence and grace not as some far off distant geographic locale on an ever-extending horizon, but right here and now.

Holy listening means then that those who call themselves Christians will not only speak of a reverent love for God's Word, but, more importantly, will give expression to this love in a willingness to listen and embrace others with diverse opinions, beliefs, and points of view. Such listening entails conversation and an openness to learn instead of a dogmatic defensiveness whose preoccupation is argumentation. Experienced in an evangelical context, holy listening is the vehicle of the Great Commission in the post-modern world where denominations and their theology must be secondary to the end to which they should point, which is Christ's love.

But the clarion call must be to move beyond superficial notions of sentimental love in order to embrace the costly love of Jesus. Once I served a church where a member finally agreed with me that she had no choice but to love a fellow church member, but she looked at me and said, "But do I have to like him?" When we are so preoccupied with giving ourselves to each other the way Jesus gave of himself for each of us, we cannot help but like each other because the costly love of service gives way to a healthy community of meaning and hope. In other words, if his love is not front and center, nothing else we think, say, or do will ultimately matter.

Daniel Aleshire observes that "Copernicus made no new discovery about the relative positions of the earth, the planets, and the sun. Rather, he put the existing data into a new structure, shifting scientific thought from a universe with the earth at its

---

[5] Ibid., 119.

center to a solar system with planets circling the sun."[6] Just as
Copernicus rearranged the data to place the sun instead of the earth
at the center of the solar system, so too holy listening requires
rearranging selfish preoccupations that include our perspectives,
beliefs, knowledge, and relationships so that divine love is at the
center of who we are called to be.

## The Simplicity and Complexity of Holy Listening

If we are willing to listen to this divine center, faith can open each
of us to the fullness of God's love. Those who have no need to
change will not profit from this book. For if there is no need to
change and if the complete dimension of truth is already known,
there is no need to listen to the faint voice of God. But for those
who have the courage and the humility to trust quietly the
confidence of their lives to the transforming will of God, learning
to listen is critical to God's way with us. Karl Barth was one of the
greatest theologians of the twentieth century whose prolific writings
resulted in over 13,000 pages of ethics and theology. But toward the
end of his great work, *Church Dogmatics*, he wrote, "We begin with
the statement that He, Jesus Christ, lives. This is at once the
simplest and the most difficult Christological statement. Any child
can make it, but the profoundest meditation cannot master it."[7] His
observation reminds me of how simple and yet profound is the faith
journey. Listening in this book is closely tied to the presence of the
wind, which is the divine grace that gives and continues giving life.
Someone sent me a card several years ago that I have not forgotten.
The inscription simply reads, "The future is born upon the wind."
Indeed, God's future is the wind that gives voice and meaning to
each of us who are willing to let grace carry us wherever grace wills
us to be.

---

[6] Daniel O. Aleshire, *Faith Care: Ministering to All God's People
Through the Ages of Life* (Philadelphia: The Westminster Press, 1988) 69.

[7] Karl Barth, *Church Dogmatics*, vol. 4, pt. 3, ed. and trans. G. W.
Bromiley and T. F. Torrance (Edinburgh: T. & T. Clark, 1961) 39.

All of my life, I have been around music, and I appreciate so much the extent to which music can exalt the soul. My mother has been a church organist for as long as I can remember. My sister sings and is the product of classical training, and my brother plays the violin. Now the scene is being replayed in my own home with voice lessons, piano practice, violin lessons, the march of the drums, and lately, the introduction of the saxophone. I know well the pain that is endured early in learning to master an instrument, and I know equally well the joy received when the music gives way to a sweet melody.

One of the intriguing aspects of music is a transition that is created when harsh chords move toward a more pleasant sound. Chords are a combination of three or more notes played simultaneously that result in a sound that not one of the separate notes or tones could produce independently. The creation of harsh chords is something that musical theorists refer to as dissonance. Dissonance is the technique where a disquieting chord of disparate notes creates a harsh sound that is resolved in the beauty of a chord that touches and inspires the depth of the human soul. Likewise, life has its squeaks and its missteps as we walk along. Too many of us struggle with the dissonance of life and the cacophony of sounds that distract us from our meaning and purpose. We yearn for the call. We want to head home. But the noise gets us lost and often leaves us confused. Yet, the sound of grace seeks to stir. Grace's presence works to resolve. For those inclined to listen, the tone of grace wills to balm the soul's deepest needs and longings and is the means by which the dissonance of life can find resolution in God's beautiful melody of love.

The passage in Luke's Gospel that leads to Jesus' telling the parables of the lost sheep, the lost coin, and the lost son intrigues me (Luke 15). Scripture tells us that the tax collectors and sinners drew near to him to listen. Who are these people? They represent sinners like most of us. They sense their lives lacking real meaning and purpose, and they draw near to the One they believe can satisfy their deepest longing. Before they can listen, they draw near. I suspect they have moved beyond the point of asking, "Where is

God?" to the far more personal question of "Where am I?" Ever notice how in the depth of hurt, one of the first things many of us think about is "Where are you, God?" Perhaps the doubt about God's presence is voiced something like, "If there were really a God, the divine would be with me now." But how seldom do we ponder in the valleys of our lives, "Where am I?" The stubbornness of our minds and our hearts keeps us from listening to God's presence. Our pursuit of other gods keeps us from experiencing divine love. Our need to act and our need to see tempt us to build golden calves that we can tangibly worship. We get lost and lose the ability to hear the God who is everywhere at all times and all places, and we go in search of gods who have mountains built by human hands with human agendas. But in all our business, holy listening requires the intentional decision to draw near in order to hear, and the simple reality is that none of us can draw near to the presence of God until we focus on the divine's transforming presence and determine to listen to the voice of God's grace.

When it comes to holy listening, I write as one on the journey and not as an expert who leads the way. One of the more humorous moments in writing this book on holy listening occurred late in the process when I was up against the publisher's deadline for receipt of the manuscript. I was in a moment of creativity and was busily writing when my wife called. I could not be present because I was too addicted to my task. I kept writing ever so gently touching the keys on the keyboard and somehow thinking, "If I type quietly enough, she will not know what I'm doing." But Cheryl is perceptive. Finally, after a few minutes of conversation, she quietly said, "When you are through writing about listening and are ready to listen, call me." Wow! I got the message and was reminded that for all of my thoughts about listening, I still have a very long way to go.

The occasion to write about listening, however, has given me opportunity to engage in much reflection. Through the years, I have kept a journal of trials and triumphs, disappointments and hopes, places and people, lessons failed and those learned. In reading the journal entries from the last twenty years, I was amazed that the same names kept appearing page after page. I now realize that these people have helped me listen to God, and they have comforted and counseled me when I inevitably failed. These people have been the visible signs of God's grace and God's presence. Circumstances have often changed. There have been good days and days of disappointment. There have been days of hope and days of hurt. There have been days when I have written at length and days when I have not written at all, but in the ebb and flow of life, these dear friends have been the constant reminder of God's love for me and have been the means by which I have ultimately been able to hear God.

These people who have been God's grace and God's prophets have kept me honest. They have reminded me of the need for integrity and the conviction toward grace. They have been the voice helping me when I have compromised on the side of expediency, and they have responded by being God's love. What they have taught me is that there is tremendous freedom when I am beholden to grace alone. How odd it is that the doctrines of formal religion that were intended to be means to the end of divine grace are often used instead to measure people in order to determine how they think—not what measure of grace they are able to hear. Too often, faith in religion allows the majority to determine what is right, but how can God's truth be determined by a poll or by what the majority think anyway?

But Jesus, as the truth, sets us free! In the same passage in Luke 15 mentioned previously, where the tax collectors and sinners drew near to listen, I am also amazed at the infinite capacity of Jesus to love. In the parables that follow about things and people who are lost, how easy it would have been for him to cast blame. If something or someone is lost, surely there must be blame. Surely, there must be sin. Surely, the pious ought to be able to judge. But Jesus does not engage in the harsh game of judgment that formal religion loves to play. Jesus simply rejoices in love over that which was lost or that which has come home.

Holy listening is recognizing that wherever we are in life, this same Jesus seeks to love us and to rejoice when we open our hearts, minds, and eyes and decide to listen, which is the way that brings us home. This kind of listening requires honesty and effort. Listening of this sort requires the willingness to search. Humility is the rule of the day. Trusting God and each other is integral to the task. But such listening has its rewards, as it is the key that opens us to the deep mercy of God.

Sadly, the Christian church is now an institution divided over terms like "conservative" versus "progressive" in matters of theology and "inerrancy" versus "inspiration" in its reading of the Bible. How ironic that our lofty words of theology and our worship of the Bible carry us no closer to the community of love and forgiveness that Jesus intended for the church to be. The message that I have heard now in over twenty years of listening for the struggle of the soul of the church is one of human power and the unending need for attention and control, regardless of which side of the theological perspective I might be inclined to hear. The word proclaimed is that God and the divine way will suffer if the "right" way of thinking is not protected and imposed upon all who need Jesus. But where is the emphasis on the mercy of Jesus? Where is the preoccupation with his example of service and humble sacrifice? Where is the faith that listens to his call? Where is the trust in each other and in God that believes that the divine might yet will to stir something new within us? Holy listening, for those who really want to hear, is the means by which God's people are being reconciled to each other and to the divine who does speak in subtle tones. Grace's sound is the silence that supports all of life, and its voice calls us to the kingdom's completed end. Its way is for all who have the courage, the discipline, the need, and the desire to draw near and listen.

# 2

# *Why Should We Listen?*

I once purchased a riding lawnmower. Our home sat on the side of a hill in a small rural town. We occupied just over an acre of land, which was a bit much for me. Forgetting that the stresses of life are exponential to the number of things we possess, I decided a riding lawnmower would make my life much easier. The one I decided to purchase came with a service warranty and required no payment for six months, so I thought this was a fairly safe risk. Leaving the van seats at home, I headed off to the building supply store and made the purchase. I personally hoisted the riding lawnmower into the van.

The exhaustion of getting this monster of a machine into the van should have clued me into what was to come. I was so tired from just finding a way to get the lawnmower home that I did not have any energy left to cut the grass. Things quickly went from bad to worse. First, there was a flat tire. With no trailer and no service that would pick up the machine, the tire had to be removed and repaired. Meanwhile, the grass continued to grow. My fear was that the yard would soon look like a badly mismanaged wheat farm in the Midwest. Finally, with the tire repaired, I was ready to cut the grass. I perched myself on my tractor and began to work away.

I am no mechanic, but I can tell you that the sound that machine made just minutes into the thrashing was horrible. A belt had come loose, and things did not look good. I looked at the fine print on the service warranty. To my chagrin, I realized that the only company that could service the lawnmower was located in a place I had never heard of some sixty miles from where I lived.

Once again the seats were taken out of the van. The heavy piece of equipment was loaded and off I went in search of the lawnmower repairman who could help make life easier. When I arrived, he informed me that the repair was not under warranty and that it would be close to $150 for him to repair the broken parts. I suddenly remembered that I had not paid one dime on this lawnmower, that I was under no obligation to keep it, and that it had done anything but make my life less stressful. I informed him that the repair would not be necessary, as I planned to return the lawnmower to its rightful owner, which was the building supply that sold me the junker in the first place.

The repairman said I could not return it because the loose belt was my responsibility. He suggested that I pray about it, come back the next day, and do what God was telling me to do. I am no rocket scientist, but it did not take a genius to catch the hint. From his perspective, what God was telling me to do was to pay the repair fee and keep the mower. Like most of us, I try to avoid conflict whenever possible. I reasoned, "Always better not to act in anger." I agreed to think about what I was going to do. I left the lawnmower with the man and made the sixty-mile trek back home.

But the problem did not go away. In fact, the distance and the time to think only made me more upset. What kind of circus had I gotten myself into and just how irresponsible could I be? I thought, "The best thing for me is to get rid of this monster as soon as possible!" When I returned the next day, the repairman asked me if I had prayed. I responded by saying, "Yes." "What did God tell you?" he asked. I said, "God told me to take the mower back!" I hoisted this peace of useless equipment back into my van and returned it to the parking lot of the company where I had bought it. The spectacle of my dumping the machine in the parking lot brought the manager running. We had an inspired conversation, which ended with the manager basically telling me never to come back. He and I were in complete agreement. My prayer had been answered!

Or had it? Caught up in a cycle of what I thought I wanted and needed, my spiritual life became consumed with praying for what I wanted God to do. I must confess that I eventually gave in and found a used riding lawnmower that helped me manage the yard I needed to keep. Owning a riding lawnmower is not the issue. But the calamitous state of affairs that the material quest resulted in disrupted my relationship with both God and neighbor—and I am not alone. Too many of us petition God as if the divine were a grand wizard. We cajole. We appease. We speak. Sometimes we get upset. We ask, "Why me?" We tell God what we want. But do we ever listen? Real prayer is not so much the art of petitioning God concerning our wants and even our needs as much as it is seeking to understand and participate in God's invitation to be caught up in the breath of his transforming creation for our lives and our call to be servants in this world. We have heard Jesus' imperative that "you may ask me for anything in my name and I will do it," but we have not made the connection to his calling for our lives, which is to love him and be the extension of his love in our world (John 14:14, NIV). He promised to give us what we need to help fulfill his commandment. Sadly, most of us just pray for what we want, supplanting the deeper needs of the soul with the unquenchable thirst of materialism.

## Resting on the Promises

The Hebrew notion of *ruach ʿelohim* is important. Translated as the "Spirit of God," the concept is akin to the cataclysmic movement of a storm that stirs new life out of the abyss of the deep that leads to creation.[1] This Spirit is the creative word that calls life into being and distinguishes humanity from God. God's Word is potent in that the divine broods over the deep of chaos and brings about creation. He speaks and nothingness gives way to being. Creation moves from light to the firmament to the oceans and dry ground to the stars and to the sun. All that is created is named by God,

---

[1] Gerhard Von Rad, *Genesis: A Commentary* (Philadelphia: The Westminster Press, 1972) 49.

underscoring the Middle Eastern view that to name something is to be sovereign over it.[2] The supreme work of creation is calling humankind into being. The act is without analogy and represents the culmination of the stirring of the Spirit of God that speaks all that is into being.

Because the spoken word that brings forth humankind is unique, learning to listen to all that God continually speaks forth in our lives is essential. But can we hear? Following the creation of humankind in the first Genesis account is the declaration that "on the seventh day God finished the work that he had done, and he rested on the seventh day from all the work that he had done. So God blessed the seventh day and hallowed it, because on it God rested from all the work that he had done in creation" (Gen 2:2-3, NRSV). Von Rad observes that the inclusion of divine rest following creation is one of the profound contributions that the ancient Hebrew made in declaring awareness of the nature of the divine. By contrast, the Babylonian creation epic details how the chief God Marduk has all of the other gods extol him following his work of creation.[3] The ancient Hebrew understood that rest was significant not only as central to the nature of God, but equally essential to the nature of humankind. Rest was regarded as the means by which humankind might recognize the divine in the created realm. As Von Rad writes,

> The text speaks... of a rest that existed before [Adam] and still exists without [his] perceiving it... . The way is being prepared... for an exalted, saving good. Nothing of that is apparent to [Adam]. How could [Adam] be informed of this mystery?... Thus at creation God prepared what will benefit [Adam] in this life, what in fact will be necessary for him, yes, that which one day will receive him eschatologically in eternity.[4]

By underscoring rest as the link between creation and con-summation, the point is made that there is a divine reality that

---

[2] Ibid., 53.
[3] Ibid., 61–63.
[4] Ibid., 62–63.

underscores all that is. God's presence is unseen and remains unheard to the casual observer, including those who are religiously superficial and lacking any substantive conviction or faith. In the silence is found God's rest that opens us to the gracious and redeeming hand of God.

Listening to the silence of the spoken word of creation that is grounded in rest is the means to discovering something of the mystery of God that can be heard by those who have the heart and the mind to hear attentively. Rest for the divine is not to be understood as mindless activity. Neither is divine rest putting off God's calling for today on some tomorrow's list of activities. While there are occasions that warrant aimless fun, the biblical understanding of rest is inseparable from the redemptive purposes of God. Our divine purpose and God's spiritual rest go hand in hand, so that to be at rest is to be aware of God's presence in all that we do. The work of God is God's rest because God's rest is redemption. As Augustine observed, "But you, O Lord, are ever at work and ever at rest."[5] The Psalmist echoes this point in his passionate plea for the Lord to create a "clean heart" and a "new and right spirit," which can only come about through the intervention of the *Ruach* of God (Ps 51:10, NRSV). Conversely, the Psalmist reminds us to "not put your trust in princes, in mortals, in whom there is no help. When their *ruach* or breath departs, they return to the earth" (PS 146:3–4a, NRSV).[6] The Hebrew word for breath that the psalmist uses is derived from the Spirit that gave breath to Adam. God breathed life into Adam's nostrils. The psalmist offers a significant insight for the materialistic age in which we live where value and worth are equated with the products we own or the neighborhood in which we live. His reminder is that we can give our lives to things that may appear to be glorious but in the end wither away or we can open our lives to the divine rest of God

---

[5] St. Augustine, *The Confessions of St. Augustine*, trans. and introduction by John K. Ryan (New York: Image Books, 1960) 369.

[6] Hans-Joachim Kraus, *Theology of the Psalms*, trans. Keith Crim. (Minneapolis: Augsburg Publishing House, 1986) 146–47.

that generates a sense of divine purpose, worth, and calling. Rest is the redemptive work of God. To listen and participate in this rest is to be aware of the wellspring of life from which our calling originates. This spiritual dimension can give our lives the rapture of transformation and purpose even as we journey toward God. As the poet Wendell Berry observed, "The mind that comes to rest...comes to rest in motion, refined by alteration."[7]

This sense of breath that renews is related to the "rush of the mighty wind" in Acts 2 when God breathes new life into the church at Pentecost. Pentecost has its beginnings in the redeeming presence of God who promises new life through divine rest. Similarly, when Moses is in the throes of the Exodus journey and in desperate search of the ways of the Lord, God responds by saying, "My presence will go with you and I will give you rest" (Exod 33:14, NIV). And in the midst of Jesus thanking the Lord for hiding things from the wise, he invites all who are weary and burdened to come to him and he will give rest (Matt 11:25–28). One can only conclude that holy listening to the redeeming hand of God is critical and that the rest of which the Bible speaks is essential to an awareness of the breath of God that underscores all of meaningful life. Holy listening, therefore, is critical because it is the means by which we can avail ourselves of the renewed breath of God that is available in every moment of life.

*Can You Hear Me Now?*

Most of us are familiar with the ingenious mobile phone slogan that has captured the proverbial phrase used by anyone who has ever talked on a cell phone. As we travel on the highway, the frequency can sometimes fade, prompting us to ask, "Can you hear me now?" If we can accept the notion that rest is central to the way God is moving from the creation of life to its redemptive end in the consummation or fulfillment of the divine's kingdom, then central

---

[7] Wendell Berry, *A Timbered Choir: The Sabbath Poems 1979–1997* (Washington, DC: Counterpoint, 1998) 6.

to this work of grace is the proverbial question that God keeps asking: "Can you hear me now?"

The problem for us is that the demands of our chaotic lives get in the way of our ability to recognize the dependent need in every moment of existence for the presence of God. Psalm 95 is understood to be a New Year psalm and, as such, a psalm of joy that celebrates renewed faith in God's history of salvation. Verses 8–11 read: "O that today you would listen to his voice! Do not harden your hearts, as at Meribah, as on the day at Massah in the wilderness, where your ancestors tested me, and put me to the proof, though they had seen my work. For forty years I loathed that generation and said, 'They are a people whose hearts go astray, and they do not regard my ways.' Therefore in my anger I swore, 'They shall not enter my rest'" (NRSV, Psalm 95:8–11).

At issue in this time of New Year joy is whether the present generation will follow in their ancestors' stubborn ways. *Meribah* means "quarrelling" and *Massah* means "testing." The great question is whether they will hear the voice of God and find their rest both from ceaseless wanderings and in arriving at home in the Promised Land, or will they continue to quarrel with each other and with God? Will they continue to test the divine by insisting on their own selfish ends? Or will they leave restlessness and strife behind in order to be opened to the Sabbath rest that Psalm 95 promises?[8] Interesting too is that the book of Hebrews draws upon this psalm's invitation to rest and states that because the wandering Hebrews of old were unbelieving, disobedient, and hard of heart, they could not experience the rest of the Promised Land. Building upon the lack of faith characterized by those who followed Moses, the writer of Hebrews accentuates the need for faith in Jesus Christ lest the disciples' fate be a similar one to that of their ancestors. For the writer of Hebrews, the conclusion was clear: those who hear the voice of Jesus and commit faithfully to him will in fact make every

---

[8] See Artur Weiser, *The Psalms: A Commentary* (Philadelphia: The Westminster Press, 1962) 624–27. Also see Exodus 17:1–7 and Numbers 20:1–13.

effort to find rest and will persevere to the end (See Heb 3–4). But significant is how the writer of Hebrews moves beyond the special dimension of a Promised Land. He connects the idea of rest to the Sabbath of creation and joins the event of creation to the consummation of life through faith in Jesus Christ (cf. Heb 4:4; Gen 2:2). More than the cessation of work, central to the rabbis' teaching of Sabbath rest was their awareness of its containment of a foretaste of the Messianic age to come.[9] Likewise, the writer of Hebrews invites people of faith to experience the rest of Sabbath that in reality is embodied in Jesus Christ. Far more important than physical relaxation is the awareness of the soul's need to be quieted in order to hear the voice of Jesus Christ as it sustains in the present and guides the pilgrim toward wholeness in the fulfillment of the eschaton. From this biblical perspective, the embodiment of creation, redemption, and consummation is in Jesus Christ. No wonder then the Bible places such an emphasis on being able to hear his voice!

But we do not listen. Central to the experience of holy listening is the awareness of God's love as central to all that we think, say, and do. Unfortunately, the tendency for many is to postulate our righteous wisdom from some self-appointed throne when what is really needed is for those of faith to be the sense of presence, hope, and trust that enables people to grow gradually in grace and holiness. Granted, our society likes to struggle with the big sins of life. We consume ourselves with issues related to human sensuality. We pride ourselves on our biblical knowledge and our pious doctrine. But we give too little attention to the far more acute need to focus on human spirituality and humility. We are inclined to emphasize individual impropriety because we are uncomfortable confessing the utter state of fallenness, which is the human condition common to us all regardless of denominational affiliation, political affiliation, theological persuasion, sexual orientation, social and economic class, or geographical location. We pick and choose

---

[9] William G. Johnson, *Hebrews: Knox Preaching Guides*, ed. John H. Hayes (Atlanta: John Knox Press, 1980) 29–33.

biblical texts to support our position and comfortably condemn whatever it is we do not understand. We simultaneously ignore other passages that are equally critical of what we have come to regard as personal habits, never contemplating the extent to which our actions might be an affront to God. Too many of us want to know whether the individual next to us is conservative or liberal. Too few of us care to reach out beyond such fabricated lines of demarcation to desire genuinely to be the neighbor's keeper in a real world where God does not give us a choice about who our neighbor will be. We preoccupy ourselves with the question of when Jesus is going to return and fail to obligate ourselves to the task of being the hands, heart, feet, and eyes of Jesus in a hurting world desperate for the experience of his love. Where any one of us can be placed on the theological and political spectrum of meaning has become far more important than how we can communicate with each other and help each other address the cataclysmic presence of evil that seeks to divide, destroy, and negate the loving presence of God.

## The Condition of Sin

Particularly acute in Western civilization is the importance of the individual. And because we tend to think of sin and salvation in individual terms, the biblical emphases on the Fall has been minimized. In a systematic context, fallenness refers to the various biblical narratives where humanity has separated itself from God. While most would readily refer to the Fall of Adam and Eve, to be faithful to scripture, fallenness has legion forms. I am indebted to E. Frank Tupper for broadening my understanding of the Biblical Fall and for accentuating the various ways in which fallenness impacts every facet of life.[10]

First, there is the concept of vertical fallenness characterized in the poignant description of the sin of Adam and Eve that led to a

---

[10] E. Frank Tupper, "Lectures on Fallenness," (lectures, Southern Baptist Theological Seminary, Louisville KY, spring semester, 1987).

removal from the garden and their intimate association with God.[11] When we think of fallenness, most of us return to the biblical story as the basis for our understanding. But there is too little reflection on where in our lives the decision was made to go our own way independent of God. We think of fallenness in the big sense, but spend too little time thinking about it in terms of our personal context. Were we to do so, each of us would be far more humble in our attitude toward others.

Recognizing that each of us has fallen is central to this book. Before one can engage in the great work of holy listening, one must recognize the propensity of the human condition, of yours and mine, to sin. Augustine's awareness is central when he prayed, "Let me confess, then, what I know about myself. Let me confess also what I do not know about myself."[12] If one assumes that their theological or political point of view is correct and cannot recognize the vast mystery of God that limits our own perspectives as well as necessitates our reliance upon absolute grace, then one will not be able to appreciate the effort and humility required to engage in holy listening. What ultimately binds us all is not our moral or ethical perspective, but our fallenness and our need to hear the word of divine grace both as we receive salvation and as we grow in holiness. Where we cannot be humble, we are no different than the Pharisee. His righteousness gave way to judgment. In doing so, he condemned himself. Likewise, where humility is not central to faith, the publican's prayer for "God to have mercy on me a sinner" remains foreign to our self-righteous awareness of ourselves in relationship to the divine (Luke 18:13). If we are not humble, we cannot hear God.

---

[11] See the biblical illustration of the vertical fall in both the Adam and the Pauline Traditions where the reference point is Adam. He is the focus of the individual's fall in relationship to God, which is accompanied by a failure to trust in the providence of the divine. Compare Genesis 3 with Romans 5.

[12] St. Augustine, *The Confessions*, 233.

Second, the Bible emphasizes the hazards of horizontal fallenness. We are responsible for our brother and sister. In Jesus' way of thinking, the story of the Good Samaritan reminds us that we are called to answer the lawyer's question, "Who is my neighbor?" He begins by observing how the priest and the Levite, having no doubt done their religious duty, were too preoccupied to stop, even though these are the two that any devout Jew of Jesus' day would have insisted be the heroes of the story. But what Jesus does next highlights the urgency for us to be connected to each other if we are to hear the heart of God. He identifies a person from a race who was the most despised by any Jew. Good Samaritan was an oxymoron. No group was more hated and considered more unacceptable to the devout Jew. And yet Jesus uses a Samaritan as the star of the story. In doing so, he teaches us not only what it means to be a good neighbor, but also about genuine love, the kind of love that represents the heart of God. Jesus is preoccupied about a way of living that is etched in the heart, mind, and eyes of those who are called to follow. He is focused on hearing the needs of the neighbor as the needs of God and his boundaries are not easily defined by somebody who looks like him. Neither should our neighbor be defined by those who look just like us. Equally true is the fact that neighbors are not just those who we consider our friends or those who think or believe necessarily the same as we do. The neighbor for Jesus is the one in need (Luke 10:25–37).

Central to the writing of the Johannine correspondence is the rejoinder that we are not to be like Cain, but rather to love our brother and our sister, whoever they might be (Compare Gen 4, 1 John 3:11–12, and John 13–15.). Cain's problem was one of jealousy. That God would show blessing on another's sacrifice sent him into a downward spiral. Cain's sacrifice did not receive the kind of attention that God displayed toward the sacrifice of his brother, Abel. Why the Lord had no regard for Cain's offering is a mystery the story does not resolve (Gen 4:5). The story does remind us of the need to take joy in the blessings of another. Being my sibling's keeper entails my hope, trust, and desire that they succeed. Such a perspective is the servant's focus. Desiring the joy of another is central to holy listening. But wanting the neighbor to succeed requires much discipline because our instincts for survival and the need to be noticed make it difficult for us to be preoccupied with rejoicing over the good that comes to others.

Third, the Bible has an explicit concern for corporate fallenness. In this context, the image of the Fall is not placed on the individual but rather upon the structures of order that give society cohesiveness and integrity (Compare Gen 6–8 and 1 Pet 3:8). Ours is a time replete with chief executive officers and chief financial officers who manipulate the books in order to benefit from the bottom line without regard for their impact on employees in particular and more generally on society as a whole. Look no further than Enron, WorldCom, and Tyco to get a picture of how would-be trusted leaders deceived their shareholders in an attempt to create a mirage of financial health sufficient for them to amass great wealth.[13] Similarly, too many politicians focus on the good of the few and too often align themselves with whatever position they believe can keep them in power instead of acting on the basis of integrity and principle. Such corruption may be even more grievous than individual fallenness because it is not as easily recognized and its systemic grip on every institution and individual, including the church, is too readily ignored.

Fourth, the emphasis on the fallenness of community is characterized in the disruption of community resulting from the tensions at Babel in Genesis 11 and the Spirit that seeks to create community at Pentecost in Acts 2. Perhaps the ultimate sin of all is the ego that seeks to usurp the place of God. How often do we act in such a way that our pronouncements result in labeling those with whom we differ? When have our words created division and discord? When we have behaved so, we have joined the great throng of believers who thought that if the tower were built just high enough, they could, of their own accord, enter the realm of God. What Pentecost makes clear is that in contrast to such

---

[13] See Jim Wallis, "Where Do Enron Executives Go to Church?" *SojoNet 2001*, 17 January 2002 <*http://www.sojonet*>.

grandiose visions of the human ego, God's voice alone can bring about community.

Observe that Jesus' commands to love God with all of one's being and to love neighbor as oneself stand in complete contrast to the forms of fallenness understood as vertical, horizontal, corporate, and community fallenness. There is a simplistic way of understanding the encompassing love of Jesus that addresses each of these forms of fallenness. The nadir or lowest point of the human condition can only be overcome by connecting to the vertex or highest end of God. But this chasm cannot be traversed apart from the equally significant need to reach beyond ourselves and connect with others. By recognizing that the vertical call to embrace God intersects with the horizontal call to love neighbor, a cross of redemption can be formed that also creates a circle of meaning. The journey of redemption that the horizontal and vertical origin creates cannot occur apart from an awareness of our connectivity to each other and to God, which includes personal, corporate, and communal manifestations. The Celtic cross pictured below perhaps best symbolizes the connectivity of God to each of us and of each of us to each other made possible through the sacrificial love of Jesus Christ.

While the relativism that is a part of our postmodern world encourages little talk about sin, the reality is that our capacity to sin must be acknowledged in order to be open to the fullness of God's grace both as individuals and as the community of faith. The trouble is that whenever we mention sin, the tendency is to think of somebody else. We assume sin is foremost for the ungodly. It is their problem. But before the church can confront the siege of sin in the world, those of us who call Jesus Christ Lord must first acknowledge our own sin. That which we must first confess is our desire to be God, which is really our desire to be the maker of our own destiny. Secondly, we must recognize the more common forms of sin like laziness, stupidity, ignorance, and stubbornness.[14] The unconscious but prevalent ingratitude for the agape love of God revealed and freely given in Jesus Christ needs to be recognized as well. Thinking of sin this way reminds each of us of our own shortcomings and our need to confess where we have failed. Herein is the invitation to humility so necessary to hear God. As Karl Barth observed, "Sin may have different dimensions and aspects, but it is a single entity.... The sin of [humanity] is also not merely heroic in its perversion. It is also ordinary, trivial and mediocre."[15] C. S. Lewis underscores the ordinariness of sin in his classic book, *The Screwtape Letters*. He writes:

> You will say that these are very small sins; and doubtless, like all young tempters, you are anxious to be able to report spectacular wickedness. But do remember, the only thing that matters is the extent to which you separate [the person] from the Enemy. It does not matter how small the sins are provided that their cumulative

---

[14] See Karl Barth, *Church Dogmatics: The Doctrine of Reconciliation*, ed. and trans. G. W. Bromiley and T. F. Torrance (Edinburgh: T. & T. Clark, 1958) vol. 4, pt. 2, 403. Barth speaks of promethean sin, which refers to our desire to be God. Prometheus tried to steal the lightning from Zeus for his own use, which Barth uses as a metaphor to describe the human desire to be God instead of a servant of the Lord. The promethean form of sin is catastrophic for the human condition, but so too are the other more commons forms of sin like stubbornness of which he is equally concerned.

[15] Ibid., 404.

effect is to edge the [person] away from the Light and out into the Nothing. Murder is no better than cards if cards can do the trick. Indeed, the safest road to Hell is the gradual one—the gentle slope, soft underfoot, without sudden turnings, without milestones, without signposts.[16]

In the context of this gradual understanding of sin, not only do our willful and arrogant actions condemn us, but our inaction to be the love of Christ condemns us as well. Sadly, too many in the church who are convinced of their own righteous holiness fail to embrace completely Jesus' fundamental command that we love each other as he loves us (John 15:12). Such love results from a disposition of humility borne of our awareness of our propensity to sin. Central to redemption and to the work of holy listening then is acknowledgment of sin and the commitment to love authentically and sacrificially even as Jesus loves and accepts each of us.

## Moving from Shadows into Light

In the play, *The Beauty and the Beast*, there is a moving scene where Belle commands the beast to move into the light. Instinctively, we are afraid of things we cannot see and of that which we cannot understand. Too often, what we fear drives our faith rather than the joy and trust of the One who wills to give us rest. Henri Nouwen writes, "People who have come to know the joy of God do not deny the darkness, but they choose not to live in it. They claim that the light that shines in the darkness can be trusted more than the darkness itself and that a little bit of light can dispel a lot of darkness."[17] Nouwen further observes there is a parallel that can be drawn between the tensions of light and darkness and those of joy and cynicism. Imperative is the need to risk by moving out of the security of our self-imposed darkness to receive the light from which God speaks. Such movement is essential to redemption and

---

[16] C. S. Lewis, *The Screwtape Letters* (New York: MacMillan Publishing Company, 1961) 56.

[17] Henri J. M. Nouwen, *The Return of the Prodigal Son: A Story of Homecoming* (New York: Image Books, 1994) 117.

to the need to ensure that hearts are kept from being bound by a
self-imposed cynicism that blots out the joy so necessary for resting
in God.

Caravaggio; *The Supper at Emmaus*; 1601 (National Gallery, London)

Caravaggio's *The Supper at Emmaus* is a wonderful painting
that portrays the tension between darkness and light. The painting
portrays the yearning to cling to that which is behind while
simultaneously being drawn to participate in the dawning of a new
light. Notice the character standing in the back on the left. He
wears the scarlet cloak and has been historically interpreted as the
innkeeper. He is an individual on the outside of faith whose calm,
dispassionate face reveals one who does not embrace Jesus. But I

cannot help but wonder if the artist wants to convey more. The scarlet cloak perhaps is suggested to point to the blood of Jesus on all who do not hear his kingdom of service and peace. But the larger question that should be pondered is that of the man's ultimate concern. What is his faith? What does he believe? Where do his loyalties lie?

Likewise, Cleopas has been understood as the disciple leaning forward in the chair. The leaning on the one hand conveys interest and excitement. But he clings to the chair. Notice the tattered sleeve in his garment. His faith in Jesus is not in question, but the totality of his commitment is. The anchored security of his chair and his firm grasp of it suggest a reality about so many who believe, which is the inability to let go in order to follow Jesus to places not yet fully seen or understood. Cleopas, it would seem, is uncertain if he can let go. Perhaps his fear of the unknown keeps him from hearing the experience of faith in its fullness.

Notice too the tension of the other disciple. He has his right hand grasping back toward the darkness from which he has come and his left hand extended out toward the viewer. By doing so, the viewer is drawn into the discussion and invited to sit at the table and listen.

Look closely at the bread and the fruit as symbolic signs of communion that invite all who would listen to participate in the redeeming work that Jesus Christ embodied. The fruit is blemished, indicating the sins of all, which Jesus has come to make whole. The astute observer will even notice the shadow of a fish in the lower right corner of the table, which is the ancient symbol of the Christian community. Notice too the formation of a dove in the right corner of the table. Kevin Alton, one of my students, pointed this out to me. This aspect of the painting was something I had missed even after years of examining its many features. The light centers on Jesus. His right hand parallels the left hand of the other disciple. Yet, to what is it that Jesus is inviting us? I wonder.

What Caravaggio contrasts is that the disparity of religious faith that causes one to work against Jesus causes another to be reserved in his full commitment and, yet, causes still another to recognize the existential tension in each moment of life where we stand at a threshold between darkness and light. Each in his own way believes in something, but the belief renders an awareness of contrasting dimensions of God. These contrasting dimensions in turn highlight the varying degrees to which each of the individuals is able to hear the call to complete faith that Jesus asks of his true disciples. The contrast in images also leads one to ponder the sincerity of faith and how religion and culture get in the way of hearing God. The painting powerfully evokes questions about faith and the degree to which each of us stands on the outside and opposes Jesus. Implied is the question of the degree to which we are willing to follow Jesus versus the degree to which our commitments and our understandings will darken the light that we all have been invited to embrace.

The painting also is poignant in its contrast with the biblical narrative where Jesus breaks the bread. Luke tells us that the eyes of those at the table were opened (Luke 24:30). But Caravaggio's introspective painting seems to be a bit more reticent. The bread has yet to be broken and a heavy cloud of darkness surrounds the light that places Jesus at the center of the painting. Rather than moving too quickly to have eyes that are opened, the painting begs the question as to whether or not those who look to Jesus and hear his utterances will see and understand. And this is the existential question that looms over each of us as well. What these images of Spirit and bread and communion point to is a light toward which the faithful must move and a darkness from which they must depart. Some of us are content to bask in the darkness of our self-imposed prison of arrogance, greed, self-righteousness, and self-idolatry. Others are vexed between moving toward the Christ and his voice of grace and returning to the life of our own creation. And yet others hear and experience the breath of God that renders new hope and a new creation.

## What Must We Do to Listen?

You just cannot whitewash wrongs. They have a way of bleeding through. I should have known better. We had just moved and common sense must have been left at the old place. In a week of living out of a cooler, trying to remember what box I placed where, and telling myself over and over just to be patient and think positively, I decided I would touch up the marked spots on walls in the den with a bit of fresh paint.

The problem began when what I thought was the right paint proved to be the wrong color. I realized too late that none of the wall's existing paint color remained, which meant that I was now going to have to repaint the entire den with a new color. This would not be bad at all, or so I thought. I quickly covered up the spots of darker paint that I had just placed on the wall with Kilz, thinking that the cream-colored paint that had been chosen would add a sense of warmth to the room. I hoped that my efforts at touching up the walls with the wrong color of paint would soon be forgotten. Wrong again. The darker paint kept bleeding through. I even tried spackling over the spots, which only made a bigger mess.

From my earlier story about the lawnmower, you can guess how hesitant I was to seek help. I finally did and I must have looked desperate. Generally, when I go to a fixer-upper kind of store, I cannot find any help. But this time the help found me. The assistant did not even ask if I needed help. He just said, "Man, you look like you need some advice." I began to describe my ordeal to which the gentleman responded, "You're going to have to sand everything to get back to the wall. You have to work out that kind of mistake; you simply can't cover it up."

Israel always understood its exile in Babylon as God's judgment. Through the exile experience, Israel too began to understand that it just could not cover up the collective sins of the nation. The community knew that somehow it would be God who would have to create a new heart and a new spirit within the life of the people. Recall Ezekiel's valley of the dry bones. This story is a reminder that exile and death are not the final words for a community of people searching for a way toward the Jordan and the land beyond (Ezek 37:1–14). The Spirit of the Lord took Ezekiel to a battlefield and asked him whether the dry bones of the long dead warriors could rise and live again. Knowing that this was a question that only God could answer, the prophet responded by saying, "O Lord God, you know" (Ezek 37:3). Reminiscent of the Genesis creation narratives, the prophet is commanded to speak and the bones are given flesh again. Then the prophet is commanded to let the very breath of God collect from the four winds of the earth in order that the very Spirit of God might be instilled within that which has been called to life. I do not remember the preacher's name. But I remember this text and a sermon delivered one day in the seminary chapel. By the time the preacher was through, the disparate words leaped from the text, and one could sense the very presence of God giving life not only to the ancient nation of Israel, but to me as well.

The truth is that we all know what it is like to feel empty, to hurt, to be afraid, to be lost, and to be uncertain. Exile is not just a metaphor, but a real place where we find ourselves more often than not. Despite our best efforts, the floodwaters of life overtake us, and often we do not feel in control. Forces beyond our measure drive so much of what we must react against, and we are left to feel helpless against the demands of life. Like the lone flute against a sea of brass trumpets, too often we feel that our weak voice just cannot respond against the demands of our world. We want so desperately to feel that we are a genuine and contributing part, and yet life seems to shout back: "You're not necessary"; "You're a failure"; and "You don't fit in."

In the larger picture of life, we argue with our children and they fight with us. We feel that we just cannot connect. Marriages fail. Perhaps it is something as mundane as our responding to the other driver pulling out in front of us with rage. Our perfect world gets rocked. We do not score as high on the SAT as we would like. Somebody else gets the rose or the new car or the promotion. Perhaps it is nothing more than the mundane frustration of being just a second too late to be the first in line when the new checkout counter opens and we are forced to stand for an eternity paying for the few items we need. Maybe you can resonate with the helpless feeling I have when I am late to some event in town, and inevitably I get stopped at the railroad crossing waiting for the train to pass.

Or perhaps a different point of view is expressed with which we morally object and fervently disagree.

Such moments can bring about a vexation and emptiness of the soul. Even worse, we unconsciously allow the frustrating moments to define our reality. Rather than saying we have failed at this or that, suddenly the temptation is to generalize to the point of claiming that our lives are a failure. Or perhaps it is not ourselves we label as a failure, but the other person whose actions, words, or lifestyle we find objectionable. Such a place is the valley of the dry bones. Such a place is the loneliness and isolation of the wilderness place. It is the state of helplessness where we are not in control. No longer is it an ancient story. It is real and personal. But just like a marred wall with mistakes that have to be worked out before a new coat of paint can be given, so too is the truth that whether it be a nation in exile or the emptiness of the soul burdened by mistakes, shortcomings or anger, the wilderness of our lives needs God's gracious breath and new creation.

Jesus too knew about being in the wilderness. He knew about being in lonely places. He knew what it was like to be misunderstood, to be dismissed, and to even be hated without a cause. But Jesus also knew about love and about important dreams that really make life worth living—dreams borne out of a sense of calling to love God with all of our hearts and to do in our lives what God wills for us and not what we feel we must have for ourselves. In all of those wilderness places where we need life, both as individuals and as a community of faith, the Spirit whispers grace, acceptance, and love. The divine calls us to breathe in the goodness of God's rest. We are invited to be God's redemptive voice where we give witness to the light and life that reigns within us.

There is a bumper sticker that says, "If you can read this, you're too close." The truth is that we need to be sensitive to each other; to be able to read the emotions, dreams, and longings of each other; and to understand that much of who we are is unique and yet so common to everybody else. We need to be too close so that we can be the good news of grace and care for each other in a world that sometimes takes more from us than it gives.

For all of its crudity and slapstick humor, the movie *Bruce Almighty* gets it right when God tells Bruce to quit being angry and jealous over all that did not work out according to Bruce's plan. He goes on to say that if you want a miracle, then be the miracle. And this is the calling that you and I have been asked to embrace. In all that is there is grace. New life occurs because God's love fills all those who open their hearts to the divine. God has issued an invitation to be life, to be grace, to be hope, and to be holy. This is who we were created to be. But the clanging tensions of our society make it difficult to hear. The transitions in our world dampen grace and leave us with fear. Yet God does speak. Do we hear the experience of the divine? Do we believe in God's love? Do we bask in redeeming rest? Listen. The voice of old says anew—to you and to me—"My Spirit will give you breath, and you will live again. I will bring you home, and you will know that I have kept my promise. I, the LORD, have spoken" (Ezek 37:14, CEV).

# 3

# *Listening in a Loud World*

The great hymn *We Are Called to be God's People* contains the phrase, "Showing by our lives his grace." Learning to listen to God, others, and self may be one of the most significant ways in which we can be grace to each other. But in this age of consumerism, the dominant message is the clarion call to buy, buy, and buy. Our society has become one where success is defined not so much by what possesses our hearts, but rather by what we possess. Voices abound that tell us what we need in order to be happy, to be fulfilled, to be accepted, and to be safe. We have become a brand name society. Tennis shoes will no longer do; they have to be Nike. Never mind that a car is a luxury to most of the world. Just think about Mercedes, Acura, and Lexus. We know the brands because they have taught us to associate their names with success. Consumerism has become sovereign, and we have been made to feel that unless we "big-size" everything we buy, we somehow are less than significant.

The never-ending quest of materialism is exhausting and debilitating. Yet the options are not just between having "more, more, more" and "nothing." Rather than being caught up in a rat race of the never-ending search for satisfaction, there is the opportunity to consider that we are people created in the good image of a loving God. Aristotle long ago argued that if we could determine the greatest good, we could then conduct our lives in such a way as to achieve that desired end. Jesus' take on pursuing the greatest good was that "No one can serve two masters; for a slave will either hate the one and love the other, or be devoted to the one and despise the other. You cannot serve God and wealth" (Matt 6:24, NRSV). The intent is not to condemn material success. The trouble is that the happiness that consumerism promises gets us off track and deafens our souls to the ultimate goodness that is the mystery of God. In an age that puts emphasis on entertainment and constant stimulation, there remains, as was true for Elijah, a need to hear the still quiet voice of God (1 Kgs 19:12). Waiting in silence and listening to the Spirit of God remains essential to discerning the worthy dream and vocation that the divine wills for our lives.

Samuel's story is one of the most remarkable in the Old Testament and provides a significant insight into a theology of listening. In contrast to so many others who had "Damascus Road" kinds of experiences, Samuel is a testimony to what John Claypool has described as an evolutionary faith that reveals a life marked not by upheaval and tension, but rather of faithful service borne out of his simple response, "Speak, for your servant is listening" (1 Sam 3:10, NRSV).[1]

His journey toward faith begins even before his conception with a heart-broken woman named Hannah. She had no children and lived in a day that lacked the explanations of modern science. The text assumes that God had closed her womb. But she prayed. She kept praying. The story tells us that Hannah's lips moved, but she did not speak because she prayed with words in her heart and she had the courage to believe that God would listen. If God would only hear her cry of despair and grant her a son, she would in turn dedicate the child as a priest to God. In contrast, Eli the priest could not hear Hannah's prayer. He was tempted to dismiss her as a crazed, drunken woman. The priest's inability to hear more poignantly symbolized the deterioration of Eli's priesthood.

The faith narrative informs us that God gave Hannah and the future nation one who would hear and obey. She delivered Samuel, which means, "God heard" to the priest, Eli, who dedicated him to

---

[1] John Claypool, "Samuel: Crossing Where It's Narrow" in *Glad Reunion: Meeting Ourselves in the Lives of Bible Men and Women* (Waco: Word Incorporated, 1985) 76.

the service of the Lord at Shiloh. The text simply says, "The boy Samuel grew up in the presence of the Lord" (1 Sam 2:21, NRSV). That Hannah's song would mirror the marvelous words of Mary that we call the Magnificat and that this brief description would mirror the words of Luke when he notes that Jesus "grew and became strong...and the favor of God was upon him" (Luke 2:40, NRSV) speaks volumes about the esteem by which Samuel was regarded in the Hebrew tradition. There had not been one like him since Moses. As a bridge between the period of the judges and the period of the kings, Samuel united the three roles of prophet, priest, and king and became the spiritual leader of his people for over forty years. The Bible understands Samuel to be one of the forerunners of Christ who listened to his calling, understood his place, and was faithful to it all the days that he inhabited the earth. More than his ability to lead and more than his ability to anoint kings was his simple ability to listen. This sense of listening is what is so profound about the life of Samuel.

Listening to God in a loud world is necessary if our lives are to have meaning. But ours is a world full of chatter. We hear all kinds of things and know that everybody is talking, but it seems as if we talk past each other and increasingly have little ability or interest in truly hearing what is being said. Simon and Garfunkel's "Slip-Sliding Away" has too easily become the mantra for many both inside and outside the church:

> We're slip sliding away, slip sliding away.
> You know the nearer your destination, the more you're
> slip-sliding away.
> God only knows, God makes his plan.
> The information's unavailable to the mortal man.
> We're working our jobs, collect our pay,
> Believe we're sliding down the highway, when in fact we're
> slip-sliding away.[2]

---

[2] Paul Simon, *Best of Simon and Garfunkel*, Sony, 1999.

And just what we are slip-sliding toward is an increasing inability to hear the transcendent in our midst. Samuel, on the other hand, experienced the presence of God because he had a spiritual intuitiveness. This was his gift and he is the reminder of the need to listen in faith. This need to know and experience a God who calls us to experience grace, to receive mercy, to live in humility, and to have hope renders a Promised Land in the here and now for those who will listen.

But to listen to God is difficult because we have to want to hear the transforming Word. Listening takes a lot of work. Listening takes a lot of faith. And listening takes a willingness to believe that we really are children of God and that we are loved. Regrettably, many lack the courage to listen with all of their being. Prosperity is too tempting. Protecting what we have, controlling what we possess, and being defensive toward all who might stand in the way have become prevalent in the church, in politics, and on the road toward wherever it is that we think we have to go. The pluralistic world to which we are exposed makes listening even more difficult because we are confronted daily with images and experiences that do not fit easily or neatly into the self-contained world in which we live. The world has never been smaller, and we have never been so aware of the material, cultural, political, and religious options that are ours for the taking. In this postmodern world, the difficulty of hearing the God fully revealed in Jesus Christ is acute. There are so many options among us. Postmodernity has created a world that resembles a large, crowded room with a cacophony of voices that makes it impossible to define any one single strand of meaning and understanding amidst the myriad of conversations. And yet, for the Christian there is one calling and one mission, which is to be God's love.

Why then is it so difficult to hear? Why is it that the cynical side of us raises itself and doubts the presence of the transcendent? Why is it that we keep trying to buy ourselves happiness? Why is that we just keep looking for love in all the wrong places? The reasons are legion, but what follows is an exploration of four reasons why we do not listen. First, we have become preoccupied with the authority of God's Word and our ability to dictate that authority instead of being focused on the need to embrace its call to love. Second, our natural tendency is to be the lord of our own destiny, and holy listening requires that we let God be God. Third, faith itself calls us to jump into the river of truth. Hearing the divine requires that we let the river take us to places where the end is the providence of grace. And fourth, holy listening requires that we have the courage to listen to our limits not from the point of despair but rather from the point of possibility.

### Letting the Story Claim Us

In such a world, the Bible longs to involve people in an unfolding of the truth of the narrative. The psalmist reminds us that God's Word is a Lamp to [our] feet and a light to [our] paths (Ps 119:105). As truth, the Bible is a sacrament and remains the living presence of Christ that calls us into the world. To understand the Bible as a sacrament is to embrace its power not as a static document, but as a river of truth that yearns to intersect our lives where we are in order to open us anew to places where grace wills to take us. Too many prefer to swim in a pond of static water instead of jumping into the river that leads to the vast ocean of grace. In this context, the Bible is the place where we encounter God and where the divine speaks, not *ex cathedra*, but in the ordinary experiences of our lives. The Bible yearns to breathe insight into our respective journeys and invites each of us to receive grace and acceptance so that we can be grace and love to others. Of profound importance for those who have the courage to listen is the opportunity to be transformed gradually to a point of redemptive love beyond anything ever thought possible. To listen to the divine is to be opened to a source of vitality that gives life meaningful purpose in terms of who we become borne out of what we do in our service to others. This center of being to which divine listening awakens is the wellspring of God's Holy Word from which we become the incarnation of Christ to others.

Regrettably, the power of the narrative to engage the believer in truth is sometimes lost. Some have reduced the biblical narrative to a literary genre of ancient myth and symbol that, while perhaps evoking a sense of renewal, nonetheless fail to embrace the life and work of Jesus Christ as imperative for salvation. The historical events themselves have been separated from the narrative of truth and are interpreted strictly in a symbolic context. The power of symbol should not be dismissed. But scripture is a strange amalgamation of historical events and meta-historical events that immerse God's self in time and, consequently, transcend time toward mystery. Christian symbols are grounded in history and, through history, have the potential to provide understanding of God's mystery that is otherwise closed to us. The power of symbols is that they point to Jesus Christ as God's participation in time.[3] To speak of scripture's value only in allegorical terms completely misunderstands how the events to which scripture testifies transcend time through the God who has chosen to immerse the divine in time.

Hermeneutics, the task of drawing meaning from ancient scriptures in order to understand the relevance of the sacred texts for today, has erred at times as well.[4] To be fair, the tools of biblical criticism have contributed much to our understanding of the Bible. Paleography, or the study of ancient manuscripts and writing habits, has helped to reconstruct what the original biblical authors intended to express by classifying over 5,000 hand-copied Greek New Testament manuscripts according to content of the material, kind of script (cursive, block letters, etc.), and date.[5] Such scholarly research resulted in the discovery in the late nineteenth and early

---

[3] See Paul Tillich, *Dynamics of Faith* (New York: Harper Torchbooks, 1957) 42–43.

[4] For an excellent and objective discussion of biblical inspiration, biblical criticism, and biblical hermeneutics, see James Leo Garrett, *Systematic Theology: Biblical, Historical & Evangelical* (Grand Rapids: William B. Eerdmans Publishing Company, 1990) 1:108–54.

[5] See Dennis C. Duling, "Interpreting the New Testament" in *The New Testament: History, Literature, and Social Context*, 4th ed. (New York: Wadsworth, 2003) 60–80 for an excellent summary of the value of biblical criticism.

twentieth centuries of earlier manuscripts that led to more accurate translations. But the scholarly approach to the Bible has at times also treated biblical truth as esoteric knowledge to be deciphered by and trusted only to the minds of the experts. The risk of hermeneutics and the scholarly study of the Bible has sometimes been a losing of the forest due to a preoccupation with individual trees. Too often, scholarly studies of scripture have left the individual standing on the outside of the text. Perhaps the student has learned to dissect the text analytically, but they have not been able to connect the objective study of the subject to the practical experience of participation in the divine work of grace that transforms culture. The purpose of scholarly study of the Bible and the New Testament in particular should be to highlight Jesus Christ's call to love God, self, and neighbor. Where scholarly studies obfuscate this clarion call, the results of the analysis are esoteric at best.

In contrast are others who rely too heavily on a literalist approach. They deny the need for study unless it relates to a system of "proof texting" that uses scripture to validate some preconceived concept of truth. When the Bible is read and studied this way, the primary intent is not transformation but rather defending what one already believes to be true. In this system, the Bible is the means by which one confirms what one already knows instead of being the vehicle that opens one anew to the infinite mysteries of God. Such individuals spend relentless energy defending scripture because they want so much for the Word to be the ruling factor both in their lives and society. Their intentions are noble. But their framework that defines scripture as being inerrant is flawed. Imperative is the need to protect "the truth" of the inerrant Bible at all cost. But what is often lacking from this perspective is any willingness to allow for critical reflection or discernment, which is so necessary for holy listening. Because they cannot fathom alternative perspectives, they lack any willingness to be opened to new insights. Having built a doctrine of scripture that is static rather than dynamic in perspective, their notions of truth lend too easily to a sense of repression. But what the Gospel invites people to is a sense of freedom where the Spirit comes from heaven rushing in like a strong wind that renders new life, new calling, and new conviction for those who have the heart, mind, and ears not just to hear, but to listen (Acts 2:2).

Regrettably, those who mean well in their defense of scripture unintentionally create a mechanical construct of faith where the still small voice of God is supplanted with a pre-determined right view of truth. In granting themselves the power to dictate their understanding of truth and in limiting their need to listen anew, a spiritual environment is constructed that makes it difficult for grace and trust to flourish in a way that allows the soul to be awakened to the kind of Christian freedom Paul spoke so eloquently of in his epistle to the Galatians (Gal 3:5). Forgetting that scripture says nothing about inerrancy, the question often asked is "do you believe in an inerrant Bible?" when really what is being asked is "do you believe in my literal understanding of it?"[6] Sadly, those who insist on an inerrant view of scripture in fact supplant the authority of Jesus with their own authority.

But there is a far richer way to interpret scripture. When Jesus speaks of turning water into wine, the narrative's truth is not in the literal act, but in the invitation to recognize that in Him is the gift of new life (John 2:1–11). Similarly, when Matthew tells us that even Solomon was not as glorious as the radiance of the lilies, the figurative language is intended to convey a larger truth, which is the beauty and value that God holds for each of us (Matt 7:29). Interpreting scripture through an understanding of its value as "historic" metaphor allows the individual to participate in a deeper dimension of truth than that allowed by inerrancy. The anchor of literalism is safe. Letting go and trusting in the power of the metaphor requires a willingness to participate in ongoing transformation. And heaven forbid that we should change our ways,

---

[6] For the Bible's own affirmation of its authority, see 2 Timothy 3:16 and 2 Peter 1:20–21. Insistence upon inerrancy forces the Bible into a framework of interpretation that is not faithful to scripture's word about itself.

customs, and beliefs just because the silent voice of God is inviting us to participate in transformation!

At issue is the need to have faith in the Word of God that frees us to participate in the world as the incarnation. To speak of metaphor is offensive to some because their understanding of metaphor suggests that somehow the Bible is not true and that the events to which the Bible testifies did not literally happen. But I am using metaphor in the sense that God's Word, if it is truly God's Word, is the Word for all times and places, which means that its power is not limited to just the past but is vitally significant for the present as well. The biblical text comes to us from another time with a worldview foreign to our own. The written Word is a witness to the key players, events, and times that shaped the biblical drama, but as a witness it also testifies to the larger story of God's reconciling the world through Jesus Christ. This is the drama of redemption that seeks to include each of us and to envelope all times, people, and places into its unfolding narrative.[7] To interpret scripture in a literal framework, as inerrancy does, is like forcing a jumbo jet in a twin-engine hangar. At issue is not the need to memorize facts as if, for example, the drama of the creation story could be reduced to a list of inerrant data, but rather to embrace the wonderment of the truth of the God of love who chose to create life and called it good.

Interpreting the authority of scripture as metaphor grounded in time means then that we must interpret it the way writers of scripture interpreted the activity of God, which is to understand it as emerging promise. Just think how the covenant with God changes from the Old Testament to the New with the birth of Jesus Christ. His life changes everything because his life is not bound by time, but rather transcends it. Achtemeier writes regarding the present relevance of the Bible, "Jesus of Nazareth became something more than a time-bound individual with the event of his resurrection from the dead. If he was the Word of God as Jesus of

---

[7] See George W. Stroup, *The Promise of Narrative Theology: Recovering the Gospel in the Church* (Atlanta: John Knox Press, 1981) 248–53.

Nazareth, he is the Word of God as Jesus Christ, risen and regnant. As such, he can continue to communicate to us God's Word for our situation."[8] By emphasizing the interpretation of scripture through metaphor, the intent is to highlight the need not to just believe in God's Word, but to participate in its transcending mystery.

Mathias von Grünewald, *The Large Crucifixion*; c.1510–1515 (Isenheim Altarpiece, Musée d'Unterlinden, Colmar, France)

Such participation is what the Apostle Paul meant when he observed the need to present our bodies as living sacrifices that lead to a transformation by the renewal of the mind (Rom 12:1–2). Mathias von Grünewald's, *The Large Crucifixion*, conveys the truth of scripture to which we are invited to participate. Grünewald

---

[8] Paul J. Achtemeier, *The Inspiration of Scripture: Problems and Proposals* (Philadelphia: The Westminster Press, 1980) 164.

portrays John the Baptist holding a small cross and a chalice standing before the crucified Christ. As he stands, he holds open a Bible uttering the words, "Behold the Lamb of God who takes away the sins of the world." But the gaze is not at the crucified Christ, but toward the viewer almost as if he is inviting those inclined to listen to join in the unfolding drama of redemption. Such an image is the invitation of the narrative, which is to join in the work of Christ and his love for humanity.

In discerning a theology of listening, paramount is the need to co-mingle the doctrine of scripture with the reality of life in such a way that we begin to talk about the relevance of God's Word from the standpoint of our participation in a life of service to the cross. The need is not so much to get back to some underlying truth that is etched in history's past. Rather, the scriptures themselves seek to propel us forward in the journey of living. They do so by confronting us, challenging our perspectives and our choices, and, in the process, drawing us into conversation with a living God experienced definitively in the life of Jesus.

*Letting the River Carry Us*

Understanding that the biblical narratives claim to propel us leads to another reason why listening for the presence of God is difficult. We fear what God wills of us and wants us to become. Carol Younger writes, "Still drenched by the waters of new life, our baptism continues. The question is, "Will we stay in the river and learn to ride the current?"[9] The Apostle Paul understood the beauty of the river of truth when he wrote: "Don't copy the behavior and customs of this world, but let God transform you into a new person by changing the way you think. Then you will know what God wants you to do, and you will know how good and pleasing and perfect his will really is" (Rom 12:2, The New Living Translation).

As vessels of truth, change involves risk. Likewise, the invitation for those willing to listen is to venture out in faith toward

---

[9] Carol Younger, "Swimming with the Prophets," in *Prophetic Ethics: Christian Reflection*, (Winter, 2003) 70.

a new horizon. Just as ships were not built to stay in the harbor, people of faith are called to be transformed in order to become our full creation in Christ Jesus. Holy listening invites the opportunity to open ourselves to new understandings of God and the Divine's love for each of us. Just as the Spirit stirred salvation's waters the first time we opened our hearts, minds, and lives to Jesus, there too is the opportunity to have those holy waters stirred again. But each of us must be willing to listen to the soul's calling, step out in faith, and walk toward and work in the holy places where God dwells and asks us to be.

What courage it must have taken for Samuel to confess God's direction before Eli and yet because he did so, scripture tells us that none of his words fell on the ground (1 Sam 3:15–21). Because he listened to God and pursued the wisdom of God all his days, his life's effort was not wasted. As the old preacher used to say, he knew how "to keep the main thing the main thing." Samuel realized the value of a life that listens to God and his faithfulness became central to God's handiwork amidst the Hebrew people. That Samuel was willing to listen meant that he was afforded the grace to grow gradually in eternal happiness whose wisdom is only discerned by a willingness to pray, reflect, meditate, and ponder both with regard to the use of his mind and his heart.

The trouble is that too often and too easily we are pressured into becoming something that in fact may appear to be quite successful from the world's point of view, but can leave us feeling alone and utterly useless. Having given all our energy to our work, to significant others, or even to the church, there is no energy left just to listen quietly to the needs of the soul and its yearning to become the child of God that we were created to be.

Once in seminary I spent a good bit of time burdening a professor with what I wanted to do in life. He listened respectfully and waited patiently. When I had finally finished, he quietly responded by saying, "You have told me what you want to do. Now what I want you to think about is what is it that God wants you to do with your life." The truth is that I had spent an inordinate amount of time thinking about what I wanted to do and very little time listening to the yearnings of the soul and the still small voice of God. Such listening takes time. Living the question of who God want us to be is the starting point from which we can listen. Becoming less preoccupied with telling God our wants and our needs and being content just to sit in silence is the wellspring from which we can begin to live the great questions of faith and from which we can begin to be transformed into the person we were created to be. Parker J. Palmer characterizes such reflection as the gift of listening to your life.[10] Such listening can occur when we think about our life experiences and those pivotal moments that have led to transition and to a new awareness of ourselves. Listening to our lives means a willingness to learn from our mistakes and failures as well as our accomplishments and aspirations. Listening to our lives means being willing to make choices that lead us to more awareness of God's love and enlarge our capacity to be that love. And listening to our lives means a willingness to see how our story intersects with the holy story of grace. For example, how is it that God is for us and with us? Do we recognize our creation in the garden, our fall from grace, our journey in the wilderness, our crossing of the Jordan, our acceptance of place, and our exaltation through Christ's resurrection to our place with God? Being able to connect our life experiences to the biblical drama is necessary in order to understand our place and our calling. Observing the thought of the Quaker Douglass Steer, Palmer notes that asking the question "Who am I?" inevitably leads to the question, "Whose am I?"[11] Having the faith to move beyond a sense of just what is in it for me to a point of discerning how God wants me to be for others is central to the art of holy listening that opens oneself to God's work of transformation.

---

[10] Parker J. Palmer, *Let Your Life Speak: Listening for the Voice of Vocation* (San Francisco: Jossey-Bass, 2000).

[11] Ibid, 17.

*Letting God be God*

To hear the call of God and to be able to listen to the Divine's initiative in our hearts, we must be willing to let God be God. But what kind of God is it with whom we have been invited to relate?

This is the crucial question. How we respond will determine how we listen and the extent to which each of us is able to hear the presence of God as well as each other. With every moment, the invitation is to give our lives completely to what Tillich referred to as the "ultimate concern" versus that which is of secondary or "penultimate concern."[12] What does this mean? When I was in high school growing up in middle Georgia, it seemed that everybody who was anybody played on the local football team. My unique gift was that I loved to kick the football and, never really caring or seeing the wisdom in getting my head knocked off, I decided the safest route for me to be a star was to pursue my dream of being a field-goal kicker. I finally made the varsity squad and became the starting kicker my junior year. I gave everything that I had and my priority was being the best kicker that I could be on the best team possible. I learned many good disciplines from the sport, but winning became my ultimate concern. The team I was on had many great athletes. We eventually won the state championship and were even ranked as the number one high school football team in America. But I remember walking off the field after my team had won the state championship thinking, "As fun as this has been, who will remember the accomplishment a year from now?" There will always be a new champion, and just around the corner, somebody else will be the headline for the day. I began to awaken to a deeper sense of spiritual need and a desire to give my life to what I believed to be the good grace of God. That was the personal starting point for a transition from a focus on penultimate concerns to the ultimate concern where I began a journey toward a more profound realization of the nature of God's grace and a yearning to live out that grace in my life.

---

[12] See Paul Tillich, *Dynamics of Faith*.

But the struggle is a constant one. We value athletes and Hollywood stars. We want to dress for success. And we are consumed with being accepted. It is the middle school mentality in a more sophisticated form. We think we are free to choose whatever path we desire to follow and more often than not the material path is the one we pursue. After all, what is freedom if we cannot choose our destiny? But in the Christian faith, freedom is given through the grace of Jesus Christ. Through him, we have an opportunity to understand the kind of God who has invited us to have a personal relationship. Christ's love is the ultimate concern both for those outside faith and those within. Where other agendas and priorities are established, listening to the divine becomes difficult if not impossible. And at this juncture, those inside the faith had best be careful lest they become like Eli's sons who had lost the ability to be sensitive to divine words only discerned through the loving heart (1 Sam 2:22–25). This danger is pervasive because the experience of Adam and Eve, which is sin, is common to all. Outside of grace, we become trapped by the web of choices for self, even if they are masked in religiosity. Outside of grace, we are not free. Regardless of whether we are the so-called saint in the pew or the sinner outside the walls of the church institution, freedom only is received when we choose to be in covenant with God, whom the Bible describes supremely as love.

Why? From a strictly Trinitarian perspective, the Father has chosen the Son, and the Son has chosen judgment, suffering, the cross, and death in order that each of us might be free in the Spirit to be transformed into the fullness of our being in Jesus Christ. A closer examination of the significance of Christ and his relevance for understanding the nature of God as Holy Love is warranted, but at this juncture suffice it to say that the invitation of grace is the opportunity to experience the divine in the most personal way. God is the ground of all that is. Conversely, the divine does not view life from a distance, but in the suffering presence of the Son, the Holy God embraces us so that we can live in the fullness of freedom that his calling provides. This choice and this way is that God has chosen to be for us in Jesus Christ. Being in him is why the

Christian is free, not to do as he or she chooses, but to be opened to the infinite measure of God and the Divine's love.

Integrally linked to this reorientation of understanding regarding human freedom is the need to reorient ourselves time and again to the God who makes us free and who has invited us to be in relationship with him. In his book, *Your God Is Too Small*, J. B. Phillips observed many ways in which we have assumed that our limited understandings of God are in fact what God is like.[13] The descriptions of ways in which God is too small are classic and include such gems as "resident policeman," "meek and mild," "absolute perfection," "heavenly bosom," and "God-in-a-box." His great insight is that we too easily and readily assume that our language and thoughts adequately convey all that there is to know about God. The result is that some embrace their finite concepts, assuming incorrectly and unconsciously that their experience of God, as good or bad as it may be, has been exhausted and that there is nothing more to be received or understood. Others choose to reject their finite descriptions of God, concluding that the Divine is nothing more than some great mythical Santa Claus.

But the biblical narrative itself highlights the God with whom we are invited to fellowship. In Mark's Gospel, Jesus prays, "*Abba*, Father, for you all things are possible; remove this cup from me; et not what I want, but what you want" (Mark 14:36, NRSV). *Abba* is an Aramaic word, which correctly translated means "daddy" or "papa." While only used this one time in the Gospels, it is significant that when in Gethsemane Jesus nears his most vulnerable moment, he utters the closeness that only a child can offer to a loved and trusted parent.

Aramaic was Jesus' everyday language, and many believe that he used *Abba* instead of the more formal *pater*, which is the Greek word for father most often used in the Greek New Testament. Like a small child who looks to his father and says, "Daddy" or "Mommy," *Abba* reveals a much more intimate relationship. As

---

[13] J. B. Phillips, *Your God Is Too Small*, 1st Touchstone ed. (New York: Touchstone by Simon & Schuster, 1997).

Frank Tupper observes, "The *Abba* experience points to the depth of Jesus' personal relationship to God throughout the entirety of his life, a relational intimacy that nurtured and sustained him in the fulfillment of his mission."[14] Grounded in love, the *Abba* Daddy God is intimately near to the Son and gives his blessing, which Tupper defines as "the gift of acceptance and affirmation, the promise of nurture and guidance."[15]

The understanding of God's nature in the *Abba* context is further underscored in the Jewish understanding of honor where everything that the father had was given to his son and, consequently, the son was expected to honor the father's name. Failure to do so was tantamount to a rejection of the Torah. As a part of the honor tradition, the son was obligated to carry on the father's work and purpose and to make the father's calling or mission his own.[16] As Jesus himself said, "I have come down from heaven, not to do my will, but the will of him who sent me" (John 6:38, NRSV).

In pondering the question, "With what kind of God have we been invited to relate?" the "Abba experience," as the theologian Edward Schillebeeckx referred to it, provides an insight into Jesus' understanding of the love of the Father and of his obligation to honor that kind of love in the world. Schillebeeckx has profoundly observed:

> God's rule...in Jesus is quite plainly rooted in a personal awareness of contrast: on the one hand the incorrigible, irremediable history of [human] suffering, a history of calamity, violence and injustice, of grinding, excruciating and oppressive enslavement; on the other hand Jesus' particular religious awareness of God, his *Abba* experience, his intercourse with God as the

---

[14] E. Frank Tupper, *A Scandalous Providence: The Jesus Story of the Compassion of God* (Macon: Mercer University Press, 1995) 43.

[15] Ibid, 41.

[16] Edward Schillebeeckx, *Jesus: An Experiment in Christology* (New York: Crossroad, 1981) 263. See also David A. deSilva, *Honor, Patronage, Kinship & Purity: Unlocking New Testament Culture* (Downers Grove IL: InterVarsity Press, 2000) 23–93.

benevolent, solicitous 'one who is against evil,' who will not admit
the supremacy of evil and refuses to allow it the last word.[17]

Out of the *Abba* experience, Jesus is able to bring a message of
hope to the world that is also a message grounded in love. This love
is inherent to the Father's nature. This love is inherent to the Son's
nature. This love is inherent in the relationship between the Father
and the Son. And this love is inherent in the Father's hope for all of
creation, which becomes the mission of the Son. Far from an
understanding of God as a grand old wizard who sits on a lofty
perch far removed from the ordinary, the kind of God with whom
we are privileged to relate is one who entered the realm of flesh,
descended to the lowliest of places, and, through the faithfulness of
the Son, has made children of all who are led by the Spirit (see Rom
8:14–17; 31–37). If God is identical with his acts, then the
transforming activity of Jesus as the Christ reveals everything about
the depth of God as holy love. One need look no further than him,
and particularly his cross and resurrection, to understand the nature
of the God with whom we have been invited to relate. Rather than
pursuing a never-ending search for the God "out there
somewhere," the invitation is to open the heart, mind, and soul to
the God who is love and to let this God and this divine love be
intimate within our being to the point that we can be incarnate love
in the world.

## Letting Our Limits Teach Us

We find listening difficult because we are afraid. Ours is a world
where it is hard to hear the love of God when there is a heightened
sense of confusion and vulnerability. On the one hand, the diversity
of the world and plethora of worldviews both within Christendom
and without confuse us. Within the church, the constant and often
angry debate about what is right and what is wrong leaves us
pondering what is real. And if it were not difficult enough to listen
because of the seemingly confused state of our society, vulnerability

---

[17] Schillebeeckx, *Jesus*, 267.

and grief threaten to overtake us because of what we cannot control. The mall used to be a place where we could escape. Now we worry about suicide bombers. We live in a world where we no longer feel protected. The boundaries of what is safe and not-so-safe have become obscured. The chaos imprisons us and the air becomes too thick to listen for the Spirit in our lives. Privately, we too are afraid because the voices that promise prosperity also remind us that without this or that we are losers. These voices remind us that we can never do enough. We can never please enough. We can never make it as perfect as we want it to be. Rather than listening for grace, the monster of fear leaves us looking for the worst, refusing to trust, paranoid of reaching out, frustrated at failed ends, and determined to rid ourselves of the chaos never considering for a moment how the chaos itself might be the seedbed for possibilities, creativity, new life, and new community. No doubt, there is a need to listen to our limits. There are some things that I cannot do and part of listening to God is coming to terms with these limitations. But learning to accept limitations is also learning to acknowledge the possibilities for my life. There is also a need to be smart about how we go about leading our lives. Jogging at night on a major thoroughfare is an invitation for disaster. But the old adage of being our own worst enemy is often true. Where we expect the worst in others and in ourselves, the worst can too readily occur. When we are angry about our past, that anger can too easily control how we choose to live in the world. In his *Thoughts in Solitude*, Thomas Merton's prayer published by the Abbey of Gethsemani underscores authentic living borne out of an ability to listen to the soul even in the midst of a journey in which the outcome is anything but certain. It is a prayer worth reading each day of our lives. He writes:

> My Lord God, I have no idea where I am going. I do not see the road ahead of me. I cannot know for certain where it will end. Nor do I really know myself, and the fact that I am following your will does not mean that I am actually doing so. But I believe that the desire to please you does in fact please you. And I hope I have that desire in all that I am doing. I hope that I will never do anything

apart from that desire. And I know that if I do this you will lead me
by the right road though I may seem to be lost and in the shadow of
death. I will not fear, for you are ever with me, and you will never
leave me to face my perils alone.[18]

To paraphrase Tillich's masterpiece, *The Courage to Be*,
Merton's prayer is an example of *the courage to listen*. Such courage
is the ability just to rest in the goodness of God's presence and
being, knowing that both in storms and quiet dullness of life, there
is one who loves us. The Divine will sustain us and will bring us to
new places of hope and understanding. Such courage is expressed in
the unshakable confidence borne out of the experience of living that
we are accepted by God, and therefore, we can live not as those in
isolation but rather as those who choose to accept each other.[19] I am
reminded of one of Gary Larson's cartoons from "The Far Side."
Two people are under the shade of a palm tree on a very small,
remote island that is just large enough for the two of them to sit.
One says to the other, "Thanks for being my friend."[20]

The truth is that ours is a small world and ours is a brief life
where there is too little time to waste on anything but being
connected to "our friends" in the larger faith community and in the
larger world of which we are a part. God beckons. God speaks. But
over against the noise of a loud world, the Divine does so not in the
flurry of a strong wind, earthquake, or fire, but in a tone too easily
obscured if we are not listening. The good news is that this voice
can be heard with resonance if we will stop and intuitively realize
that we are known by name, that we are loved, and that we are
called to a life of self-surrender where doubt, fear, and spiritual

---

[18] Thomas Merton, *Dialogues with Silence: Prayers and Drawings*, ed.
Jonathan Montaldo (San Francisco: Harper San Francisco, 2001) vii.

[19] See Paul Tillich, *The Courage to Be* (New Haven: Yale University
Press, 1952).

[20] Ronald B. Adler, Lawrence B. Rosenfeld, and Neil Towne,
*Interplay: The Process of Interpersonal Communication* (Fort Worth: Harcourt
Brace College Publishers, 1995) 238.

arrogance give way to grace. And the wonder of it all is that some of us with great gladness humbly respond, "Speak, for your servant is listening."

# 4

# *Longing to Be Made Whole*

Much has been said of the need for a personal mission statement. Ben Franklin loved to make lists. Perhaps the most famous of those was his list of personal virtues written at a very young age that he determined should define his life.[1] The "Fruits of the Spirit" in Galatians 5 compose another list about what kinds of virtues grow naturally from the heart of a person filled with the love of God. Living by such lists has value when one recognizes that in a gospel of grace, virtues are never achieved but rather are experienced through God's Spirit sustaining the believer with love.

But the art of striving to achieve the virtues of such lists can be equally detrimental. As a child, I used to love to read the book *The Little Engine that Could*. This children's story provided a source of personal motivation through my early adult years. But somewhere along the way, I realized that I was spending too much energy and time trying to "get over the mountain" and I had no energy left just to accept God's love, goodness and grace along life's way. Committed to saying, "I think I can, I think I can, I think I can," I forgot the affirmation that "I am" because God's grace simply says it is so.

More than an ability to pursue virtues, holy listening evokes an awareness of Christ's grace, which I believe to be vital to a meaningful life. We pursue constantly God's will as if there were

---

[1] See Walter Isaacson's "Citizen Ben's Seven Great Virtues," *Time*, 7 July 2003, 102/1:40–53.

some predetermined script for our lives. Yet, the grace that Christ offers is a freedom that is not preoccupied with personal choices about what to do, where to live, what to wear, what kind of car to drive, etc. Freedom of this sort is a product of a consumer world that has led us to believe that choices are essential to freedom. But the grace that Christ offers is an invitation to rest in divine love in order to be that love in the world.

A friend once told me a story of a colleague in the banking industry who fervently prayed that God's will would be made known regarding whether he should stay in one city on the east coast or move to another city on the west. In the final analysis, he decided to move. Six months after the colleague had taken the new position, my friend called to ask how he knew it was God's will that he should move. The colleague honestly replied by saying in the end he had come to the conclusion that God did not care where he lived, only that he be God's love wherever he chose to reside. This conclusion gave him the freedom to risk moving to a new place with new possibilities.

A faith that yearns to be Christ's love is a mission statement for life. When the desire to be the incarnation of love is preeminent in our mission, every other dimension of life is shaped by this faith commitment. Recall the discussion in the second chapter that emphasized the extent to which we relate to God (the vertical component) is the extent to which we will relate to neighbor (the horizontal component). The two dimensions when connected can be viewed in the shape of the cross, which is the symbol of God's agape love.

A faith that is aware of the divine presence of love has meaning for both the personal and community components that comprise our lives. At issue is how we become whole, and, as Laurent Daloz observes, "The words *heal* (sic.) and *whole* (sic.) share a common root" so that the journey that longs to be made whole is not a journey toward perfection but one toward healing.[2] At a personal

---

[2] Laurent A. Daloz, *Mentor: Guiding the Journey of Adult Learners* (San Francisco: Jossey-Bass Publishers, 1999) 148–49.

level, the invitation of faith as love is a journey toward God. At a community level, such faith is viewed as a homecoming where the people of God accept us as we are and love us into all that we can be. Understanding faith as both a journey and as a homecoming is necessary if we are to move toward wholeness and healing in a way that makes real meaning for our lives borne out of the need to receive and to be the love of God.

## The Journey through the Night

The inward journey of faith is one that beckons us to see more clearly day by day who God is and, consequently, who we are trusted to be as we love. This inward journey requires centeredness, focus, and clarity about who Jesus Christ is, who we are, and what we are called to do in relationship to him. The biblical model for such a journey is the Exodus story of the Hebrew people. Like them, we are on a journey that is comprised of a fleeing from the slavery of Egypt, a sojourn in the wilderness, and interim periods of basking in the Promised Land only to sojourn still longer in the wilderness just on the other side of the Jordan.

From a Christian perspective, this journey entails an openness of the soul to the saving experience of Jesus Christ. The awareness of the human condition apart from God and the need for the redeeming of Jesus Christ is essential. But salvation is one point on the linear movement in life that leads to truth. It is not the zenith of one's experience and knowledge of God. Regrettably, in their noble efforts to proselytize many evangelical Christians fail to put equal emphasis on the need and responsibility to recognize that an essential component of experiencing God is the movement from salvation to sanctification, which is the life of faith that receives grace, grows in the grace received, and moves gradually through grace toward holiness.[3]

---

[3] See William E. Hull's succinct explanation of sanctification in *The Christian Experience of Salvation: Layman's Library of Christian Doctrine* (Nashville: Broadman Press, 1987) 131–38.

For the one who searches, the inward journey requires no small amount of humility and a willingness to embrace our own darkness in order to experience more fully Christ's light. Recognition of the wastelands of existence is essential where the searching soul acknowledges those times when, as T. S. Eliot writes, "You cannot say or guess, for you know only/ A heap of broken images, where the sun beats,/ And the dead tree gives no shelter, the cricket no relief,/ And the dry stone no sound of water."[4] These "wastelands" are not just a part of the experience prior to a personal relationship with Jesus Christ, but loom on the shadow side of the journey and are a component of existence in our search for real life. I once asked my brother, Jonathan, who is a pastoral counselor, what was the most difficult thing about counseling. He responded, "Getting people to run toward the roar." He went on to tell a story about how when a lion gets too old to run during a hunt, the pride places the old lion opposite of the spot where the rest of the group intends to lie in wait for the prey. When the prey approaches, the old lion lets a mighty roar, and the prey, fearing the sound, runs in an opposite direction, only to run into the rest of the pride waiting to feast. The moral of the story is that the task is getting people to address those things which disturb them rather than running in the opposite direction.

Vital to the search for truth is the call of the soul to acknowledge that we do not understand everything about God's mystery. There will always remain the need to grow in Christ's grace in order to be his incarnate love. Such growth, however, is not something that is achieved. When Paul spoke of his desire to "press on toward the goal for the prize of the upward call of God in Christ Jesus" (Phil 3:14, RSV), the context for this emphasis was on receipt of the unmerited and unfathomable grace of Jesus Christ. Against those who insisted upon the Law and the performance of works as the means by which to receive God's favor, Paul understood the

---

[4] T. S. Eliot, "The Wasteland," in *The Norton Anthology of Poetry*, 3rd ed., ed. Alexander W. Allison et al. (New York: W.W. Norton & Company, 1983) 1001.

motivation of the Christian in terms of God's initiative already achieved through the unmerited and perfect love of Jesus Christ. To know Christ is to experience divine love with every fiber of our being so that pressing on toward the prize becomes a metaphor to describe the reality of pressing on to experience this grace more fully. The divine invites us to grace. A refusal to accept ourselves—limitations and all—as individuals that God has made his own can lead to depression about all we feel we should be and ought to do in the face of perfection. Conversely, human initiative can also lead the person of faith to become arrogant and judgmental toward those who have not reached the adherent's assumed state of spiritual wholeness. But the enterprise of growth that avoids depression on the one hand and arrogance on the other is the openness to reside in the vast sea of God's love and mercy. There is no need to strive for perfection—only the need to reflect quietly and wait patiently as the perfection of the Spirit stirs within us making us a new creation.

But this journey of transformation is not easy. The mystic tradition exemplified in the classic *Dark Night of the Soul* by St. John of the Cross characterized this inward search for the experience of God. He beautifully portrayed a movement from the active night, to the passive night, to the dark night, and finally to the light of love. The active night is the point at which the senses are receptive to the need for extraordinary grace of the divine. The passive night is that point along the way where the soul faces its imperfections. The dark night is the time in life when the soul is able to give way to the love of self. The dark night is a restless period in which the false sense of pride gives way to a state of quietness and peace that rests, patiently waits, and trusts in the midst of the darkness for the time in which God will enkindle the soul with the spirit of love. Certainly, the journey toward the sacred is not without sacrifice, loneliness, disappointment, failure, grief and pain. St. John of the Cross in fact believed that vexation was necessary in order for the soul to recognize its state of emptiness and its absolute need for God as highlighted in the Psalm of David who cried, "In the desert land, waterless, dry and pathless, I appeared before Thee, that I might see Thy virtue and Thy glory."[5] For St. John of the Cross, spiritual humility, which contrasted with the sin of spiritual pride, was the soul's pursuit through this journey of the nights to a recognition of misery apart from God and of delight in the gift of divine love. The ability to listen to the enkindling power of divine love occurred through the willingness to empty oneself of all sense of self-importance in order to be made whole.

This desire to grow in faith that is deep-seated in Christ's love is the source of divine wisdom that can guide each of us on the journey to greater truth. Immersed in Christ's love, we need no longer be defensive or protective of our faith in God. In fact, we can even be open to change, understanding that transformation entails greater awareness of the infinite love of God. Faith embedded in Christ's love yearns for such a journey where we do not fear or ignore the complexity of mystery but embrace it as the means of hearing anew the voice, calling, and love of the divine.

### There's No Place Like Home

As essential as the linear nature of the journey toward truth is to the pilgrimage of faith, there is equal need for oasis and rest in the wilderness. Relationships and community are necessary for transformation. The community component emphasizes the importance of home and encourages the pilgrim to seek community with others who are on the pilgrimage. Making relationships and becoming connected to a larger sphere of people whom we are called to love and who are called to love us is essential. The outward journey is the recognition that we are not alone, that we sail on a restless sea with others, and that the Promised Land is not so much a place of destination but a gift of community that we experience along life's way.

This part of the faith experience is difficult for me. Give me a task and I am as happy as I can be. There is something addicting

---

[5] St. John of the Cross, *Dark Night of the Soul: A Classic in the Literature of Mysticism*, trans. and ed. by E. Allison Peers (Garden City, NY: Image Books, 1959) 80.

and insane about getting the next task done. I like the sense of accomplishment. But people are what make life meaningful. When the energy to get the tasks done overrides the need to relate to people, the tasks themselves become a graven image that we worship. The sacred gift of friends, family, and all those we have occasion to love are in the end what make the journey meaningful. When our quest for God and our need to do God's work become so important that we fail to listen to the love of those around us, we negate a sacred component of faith at our own spiritual expense. As Sharon Daloz Parks has observed, "There's need for both detachment and connection, pilgrims and homemakers, journeying and homesteading, pilgrimage and home" in the journey of faith. Just as there is need to journey toward God, there is also need to be at home within community in order to find acceptance even as faith is nurtured.[6]

Perhaps the greatest homecoming story in the Bible is that of the Prodigal Son found in Luke 15. The entire chapter talks about things that are lost only to be found again. The joy that follows is heightened because of the appreciation gained from having experienced the absence of something loved. Be it a sheep that has gone astray, a coin that has been lost, or a son that has squandered his gifts by wandering aimlessly in a distant land, the joy of coming home is underscored. Rembrandt's *Return of the Prodigal Son* brings to life the joy of the aimless son having found a place to rest safe in the arms of his father.

Henri Nouwen eloquently describes the power of this painting. He observes that the father's left hand is strong and muscular and parallels the son's foot that is wearing a sandal. He further observes that in stark contrast is a feminine right hand that

---

[6] Sharon Daloz Parks, *Big Questions/Worthy Dreams: Mentoring Young Adults in Their Search for Meaning, Purpose and Faith* (San Francisco: Jossey-Bass, 2000) 50.

Rembrandt, *Return of the Prodigal Son*; c.1668–1669
(St. Petersburg, The Hermitage)

parallels the son's wounded foot.[7] Suddenly the painting captures for the viewer the power of the story that wills to describe the heart of God, which is a heart that is strong in the face of the storm and a heart that is gentle—always willing to accept and to heal. In recognizing both the feminine and masculine characteristic that Rembrandt accentuates in the painting, Nouwen writes:

> As I now look again at Rembrandt's old man bending over his returning son and touching his shoulders with his hands, I begin to see not only a father who clasps his son in his arms but also a mother who caresses her child, surrounds him with the warmth of her body, and holds him against the womb from which he sprang. Thus, the return of the prodigal son becomes the return to God's womb, the return to the very origins of being and again echoes Jesus' exhortation to Nicodemus, to be reborn from above.[8]

Likewise, is not homecoming to be regarded as a return to the womb? While faith is a journey, it is also returning to the place of unconditional acceptance and love. Even more poignant perhaps is the consideration of the ways in which the church, as a home, is in fact the womb from which people are being accepted, redeemed, healed, and made holy as they accept each other in the way the father accepts his wayward child who has returned home.

## Homecoming and the Work of the Church

The image of the church as the womb has its limits because ultimately the divine brings about the creation of redemption. But the church is a place where the dawning of new life occurs. Central to the biblical understanding of human creation is the view that the individual cannot be understood apart from the community or communities of which he or she is a part. To be a person created in the image of God is to be an individual within community. Humanity was created for the purpose of entering into I-Thou relationships with God and others. The Christian concept of the

---

[7] Henri J. M. Nouwen, *The Return of the Prodigal Son: A Story of Homecoming* (New York: Image Books, 1994) 98–100.

[8] Ibid., 100.

Trinity itself emphasizes the importance of community where the Father loved the Son "before the foundation of the world" (John 17:24, NRSV) and where the Spirit reveals and teaches this love to those who abide in Christ (John 14:16; 26 and John 15:10–12). The Old Testament too is replete with this sense of the communal nature of life bound by covenant where the *laos tou theou*, the people of God, are called into being for purposes of relationship in order to reveal the Divine's loving kindness to the world. And in the New Testament, this mission is extended to the church through Jesus Christ's call to be light and salt (the role of witness), to be a community of service preserved by a commitment to justice through love, and to be *koinonia*, or authentic fellowship where both grace (2 Cor 13:14) and goods (Phil 4:19; Acts 2:44–45) are shared.[9] The church as the embodiment of *koinonia* must be an oasis and a place where people feel at home and where they are loved and cared for in the great anticipation of the birth into all that God will enable them to become.

How then does the church serve as a place of acceptance and nurture? What responsibilities does the community of faith have in caring for individuals who come its way? The church as a place we can call home means that the people of God who comprise the church accept each other as they are always with an eye toward helping each other embrace God's hope more fully for our lives.

Yet, the church's responsibility as a spiritual home to offer hope and administer grace is threatened by the postmodern world in which we live. Rather than being the voice of hope, the institution feels threatened, and the sense of vulnerability and insecurity the church feels leads it to react in judgmental ways. Conflict within the community always looms on the horizon, particularly in the connectedness to other cultures and thinking and in the relativism of the postmodern world. N. T. Wright has

---

[9] For an elaboration on this manifold function of the Christian community, see Dale Moody, *The Word of Truth: A Summary of Christian Doctrine based on Biblical Revelation* (Grand Rapids: William B. Eerdmans Publishing Company, 1981) 318, 429–33.

described postmodernity as a world of neutral knowledge and truth where "everybody has a point of view, and that point of view distorts; everybody describes things the way that suits them. There is no such thing as objective truth."[10] In the postmodern world, the individual's significance lies in their ability to embrace a story in a vast sea of stories in a world that encourages a market of options and meanings. As Wright expresses it, "Scoop up what you like and mix it all together."[11] And so in this postmodern world, it is inevitable that the church itself will find disagreement. But even in the midst of disagreement, the church is called not to argue and not to divide but rather to struggle to understand its priorities. With so much to offer this world, the real temptation is to put all of the emphasis on that which separates and divides the community at the expense of embracing all to be agape love.

Conservatives and liberals alike draw distinctions that support their theological points of view. Those on the theological right want to rely on the external authority of God's Word. Those on the theological left believe that the authority of scripture needs to be interpreted in light of contemporary experience. Conflicts abound on ethical issues. Even political parties try to solicit the Christian vote by assuring us that they are the party of God. Cultural differences lead to disagreement about the role of women in ministry, including the calling of pastor, and differences occur about the meaning of biblical authority for the postmodern world. The conflict is indicative of the challenge that postmodernity creates for being a Christian community in a diverse society and multicultural world.

The debate is similar to the struggle of the early church portrayed in Acts 10 where Jewish Christians believed obdurately that Cornelius had to become a Jew first and adherent to their customs and ritual practices before he could receive the Holy

---

[10] N. T. Wright, *The Challenge of Jesus: Rediscovering Who Jesus Was and Is* (Downers Grove: Intervarsity Press, 1999) 151.

[11] Ibid., 152.

Spirit.[12] Peter knew differently and beckoned all who witnessed this new way of God's working in the world to go do what was right, which was to preach to the people that all who believed in Jesus Christ would receive forgiveness of sins through his name.

What then are we to do in a sea of change? We are to reclaim the biblical mantra that all those who call on the name of Jesus will be saved (Acts 10:44–48). Period. Ethics and theology are secondary to this biblical invitation. This is why the Jewish insistence on circumcision, which since Abraham's time had been the symbol of their identity, paled in comparison to the joy of those Gentiles who experienced Jesus as Lord.

The task of the church is to embody Christ's love and to preach his love to all who call upon him. Our preoccupation with different ways of interpreting scripture and our divisions over theology and ethics are but excuses that keep us from being God's love and from hearing his presence in our midst. None of us can speak for God. Many of the contemporary issues will only be resolved in time. Who among us today would use the name of God to justify slavery, as was the case in the nineteenth century? You see it is easy to be a self-appointed prophet condemning whatever the populace demands always under the guise of being faithful to scripture. But for most of us, the challenge and higher calling is to be God's love and leave God's judgment to him alone. As one of my colleagues brilliantly puts it, "When I get the thing about God's love figured out, I'll move on to some of the other teachings in the Bible!"

In being called to love, the local church is invited to reorient its understanding of time and to participate in an eschatological mission. In other words, we look at time as the past and the present that shape the future. But God looks at time from the future, from the kingdom's end where love is the final decree that guides all that

---

[12] See also Acts 8:26–39 and Philip's baptismal encounter with the Ethiopian eunuch.

we are evolving toward.[13] From God's future-oriented perspective, the church is invited to embrace the mission and presence of Jesus Christ. The church is called to live and not just preach his radical ethic of love. The church is commanded to sow seeds of justice and mercy. His story as the story of all stories is to be proclaimed. The Great Commission is to be realized by reaching out with open arms to a world that needs the agape love fully revealed in Jesus Christ. This way, his way, is the way in which to overcome alienation from the Divine, from each other, from ourselves, and from all of creation. The One who John's Gospel describes as in the beginning with God, through whom all things are made, and in whom is life and flesh that has dwelt among us is the One through whom we have received grace upon grace (John 1). He is the Crucified One who has been resurrected. In his resurrection, all who believe have been opened to the agape love of God. They are invited to be this love in a world that is devoid of it. More importantly, the extent to which the church can unify around agape love as opposed to judgment will be the extent to which the Christian church will remain united and vibrant in the century to come.

If the church is to provide a sense of home for those of faith, paramount is the need for the church to be agape love and grace. The ultimate realization is that we become an extension of the divine in the world. As Wright has observed, "Once we have glimpsed the true portrait of God, the onus is on us to reflect it: to reflect it as individuals and as community. Once we see who Jesus is, we are not only summoned to follow him in worship, love and adoration, but to shape our world by reflecting his glory [and love] in it."[14] In the face of all that we do not understand, such a position

---

[13] See Jürgen Moltmann, *Theology of Hope*, trans. James W. Leitch (London: SCM Press, 1967). Moltmann writes, "The Church takes up the society with which it lives—into its own horizon of expectation of the eschatological fulfillment of justice, life, humanity and sociability, and communicates in its own decisions in history its openness and readiness for this future and its elasticity towards it" (328).

[14] Wright, *The Challenge of Jesus*, 124.

is redemptive, hopeful, and essential for the church called to God's love, which is fully revealed in the life and work of Jesus Christ.

For those who call ourselves Christians, beyond the need to confess our sin is the tremendous need for churches to develop a mentoring process that is not focused so much on indoctrination but trust. The Christian community needs mentors who accept individuals as they are in order to help them foster a discipline of listening to the voice of the Divine. Needed are mentors who trust the soul to become all that God would desire. As mentor, the Christian community awakens the individual to gifts not previously recognized and provides opportunities to share those gifts in order that the individual can evolve spiritually. The Christian community exists to provide encouragement, to develop potential, and to give the individual a foundation upon which dreams of self and calling to serve can be realized.

Simply put, if a woman has been called to preach, the nurturing community will trust the individual's call as a call from God and will quickly engage in the business of nurturing the call. Immediately, there will be those who will cite 1 Timothy 2:12, which states, "I permit no woman to teach or to have authority over a man; she is to keep silent" (1 Tim 2:12, NRSV). But interestingly enough, those who would cite such a passage often overlook other passages like the one just preceding it that instructs women not to wear "their hair braided, or with gold, pearls, or expensive clothes" (1 Tim 2:9b, NRSV). They dismiss Paul's belief that in Christ Jesus there is no longer a distinction between male and female (Gal 3:28), and they ignore Peter's reference to the prophet Joel where in the eschatological kingdom to come both sons and daughters will preach (Acts 2:17). What the church ought to be about is embodying the eschatological kingdom here on earth. If both the sons and the daughters are to preach in the kingdom to come, isn't it best that the church get busy mirroring his kingdom in the present age? The reality is each of us either has a gospel based on judgment or a gospel based on grace. An understanding of scripture and the work of God is always dependent upon which pair of lenses we wear, and the lenses of judgment versus those of grace determine how we hear God in this loud and confusing world.

Those churches that insist upon selectively interpreting certain scriptures from a narrow, literal point of view while ignoring others are in the end not being consistent or faithful. They usurp the Spirit of the living Lord who determines the call of each of us regardless of gender, and they negate the gifts that the Creator has endowed upon some because the calling does not conform to their cultural interpretations of God's Word. Having spent so much time and energy arguing about what is correct and incorrect and who is right and who is wrong, such churches, with every intention of protecting the light by being defensive about it, in fact contribute to darkness.

When receiving grace in order to be grace becomes the mantra of the day, the church suddenly begins to be focused on what matters. Suddenly, there is no need to argue about doctrine and beliefs because we find ourselves too busy loving and caring for each other. Who preaches the gospel, including which gender, becomes secondary and peripheral to the desire to live out the good news of Jesus Christ's saving love. Being Christ's love takes on precedence that pales the substance of a "pure" theology. We must move beyond a preoccupation with how conservative our theology is because we are enthralled with how liberal our hearts are in the infinite need and capacity to love.

By mentoring individuals in faith development, the Christian community accepts the responsibility of encouraging its own to be the love of Jesus Christ. An unknown author from the sixteenth century wrote, "Not where I breathe, but where I love do I live." Where the inward journey by its very nature seeks to become more love tomorrow than it is today, the community balances this search to be somewhere or something else by reminding the individual that he or she is already loved by both the church and God. In addition, the community teaches us to learn to trust and work together for the common cause of being the incarnation of God's love.

## Christian Evangelism and Missions

Being a community where love is emphasized at the expense of judgment inevitably raises a question about appropriate boundaries for the institutional church in the postmodern world. The institutional church is going to have to be willing to experience a radical change in the understanding of itself if it is going to be a viable entity for the century to come. If the church is to be the incarnation of love, the institution can no longer think of itself as a sustainable organism fed by those attracted to it. Rather, the faithful must reach out into those communities and places where people, for whatever reason, have given up on church as holding any meaning for their lives. In reality, less relevant will be the orthodox boundaries of doctrinal faith and more pertinent will be the need for pliable parameters that allow the church to broaden its view of reality, even as the world becomes more connected and more aware of vying religious symbols, traditions, and perspectives. Expressed differently, what will need to be central to the Christian church in the postmodern world will be a sense of mission where the preoccupation becomes one not of denominational or ecclesiastical control, fixed theological boundaries, numbers, goals, long-range planning, building additions, ever expanding parking lots, and ministry markets. Rather, the call will be to make the incarnation of God in Jesus Christ alive in every facet of being.

For too long too many have had a triumphal notion of faith that paraded their version of Jesus. This version of Jesus is what we get caught up defending, never realizing the power of culture to mislead and confuse our beliefs. For example, I once worshiped in an African American setting. Placed around the chapel were paintings of Jesus and the disciples in the dark skin of African origin. For the first time, I realized how culture had shaped my image of God. Because of culture's powerful and unconscious sway, the church must be careful in the exclusive claim of Christ that it does not relegate God to a god primarily of Western civilization. Likewise, the Christian mission in lands dominated by other religions must rest upon the positive attraction of the person and teaching of Jesus and his love. Christian missions must influence indigenous people not by telling them they are wrong, which is a position of theological arrogance, but by embodying God's agape love that suffers and dies in order to redeem. The Christian commitment to evangelize must begin with the understanding that all, including those in the church, are broken and in need of the gift of God's grace. And the Christian commitment to mission must be for the world what Jesus was, which is a willingness to be last in order that the least of this creation might be first in God's Kingdom.

In such a commitment to Christian missions and evangelism, a relationship with the person of Jesus Christ will be more important than a set of beliefs about him. Embracing him and experiencing him as a person full of love will be the most significant impetus for being his incarnation in the world. As Brett Younger observes, "That's why the church is not about numbers, success, or institutional goals, not about human effort or clever planning. The church is about caring for hurting people and a holy self-forgetfulness on the part of the church. The church is not an end unto itself. The church is about God. God is here when we help one another and when we help people we don't know. God is here when we decide to love, hope and dream."[15]

Luke begins the church's story in Acts, and the writer's narrative concerning the call of the disciples just prior to Pentecost reveals much of what the church must be about in this postmodern age. Jesus commands the disciples to be his witnesses in Jerusalem, Judea, Samaria, and even the remotest part of the earth. I find it interesting for an age consumed with knowing signs that portend the end of time that Jesus reminds the disciples that such pursuits are folly. For Jesus, knowledge of the end of the age is reserved for the Father alone. The task of disciples is to be about the divine mission of being and revealing the love of Jesus to the remote places

---

[15] Brett Younger, published sermon titled, "Thanking God for Broadway Baptist Church," Broadway Baptist Church Newsletter, July 20, 2003.

of the earth. Luke's narrative of this commission calling helps us as well. The book of Acts, as is the Gospel of Luke, is written to an unknown individual named Theophilus. If Theophilus, which means "friend of God," is understood to be not so much one person but rather a reference to all who are friends of God, then the commission narrative can be understood as a personal invitation by Jesus to take the Gospel to the "remotest part of the earth" (Acts 1:1–8, NASB). And just as the individual is called to engage both an inward journey of the heart as well as to become at home with fellow pilgrims along the way, there are both inward and outward dimensions of Jesus' calling to the remote places of the earth. In fact, one cannot genuinely hear the outward dimension of the commission calling until one commits to an ongoing transformation throughout one's life. Most of us think of the remotest part of the earth as some place far away. But when our mission begins to be thought of both in individual and community terms, a remote place can be defined as any place where the love of Jesus Christ is not supreme.

At a personal level, the call of the Great Commission is to let the gospel of divine love penetrate the places in our souls where we are afraid, where we need to control, where we are selfish and arrogant, and where we have yet to give ourselves completely to the reign of God. We must understand that no matter who we are, no matter what we have achieved, no matter how many degrees or titles we possess, no matter the size of the church we pastor, no matter how influential the group with whom we associate, and no matter how lofty the accomplishments of our lives, there remains a need for humility and acceptance of Christ's love. Outwardly, being the Gospel in the remote places of the earth means that we cease taking for granted those we love the most and increasingly allow them access to the most intimate places of our heart. Listening to our spouses, significant others, children, and closest friends will take on new priority. Being incarnational love in the remote places of the earth will also mean being the Good Samaritan to the neighbor we know and the neighbor we do not know. Such remote environs provide an opportunity to express incarnate love in redemptive ways.

## Questions and Answers

Where faith is viewed as a transforming process in an infinite God whose love is inexhaustible, there will be a need to question and a desire to search for answers in order to make meaning of this infinite God in a finite world. Regrettably, too many view such questioning and reflective thinking as an offense to God and as an expression of a lack of trust. But, in fact, both the questions we ask and the critical receiving of answers are crucial to the life of faith. Long forgotten, but far too needed is a reclaiming of St. Anselm's notion of faith seeking understanding where that understanding is not a static set of beliefs but a dynamic activity of discovery. This process of seeking allows opportunity for each of us to open ourselves fully to the God who in Christ, to paraphrase the ancient Gallic prayer of St. Patrick, is with us, before us, behind us, and within us. Journeying from faith to faith, we relinquish insistence on doing things the way we have always done them in order to experience new dimensions of meaning. Accordingly, we will have to move to the point of seeing the church and its mission not as my mission and my church, but that of God alone. Such an understanding of faith means that we commit ourselves anew to a faith that incorporates the Spirit of transformation first in ourselves and then in others. In this way, both the Christian mission and the purpose of evangelism are to be Jesus and the wideness of his love in all those remote places near and far both in our hearts and in our world.

It is imperative that we grow in the love of Jesus Christ. But too few of us ask and even fewer of us associate the critical questions of existence that are necessary for seeking truth. The questions provide a necessary evaluation of our understanding of God. Questions help us explore the richness of faith and require honesty in the earnest desire to experience the depth of God's wisdom and love. Questions require that assumptions of faith be analyzed and that new dimensions of faith be received when the assumptions are no longer valid. Simply put, questions enliven our ability to be aware of the presence of God and the dimensions of meaning to which God calls us.

What are the critical questions? Asking questions like, "Who am I?" "Who is God?" and "What am I to do?" are fundamental to the journey. Even asking the question, "Why, God?" is often a necessary component of the process by which we begin to understand the ultimate purpose of the trail we are blazing. But as Sharon Daloz Parks has written, "I have observed, among some of the most talented [students], many who simply have been lured into elite careers before anyone has invited them to consider the deeper questions of purpose and vocation. Others are fiercely determined to find a distinctive path and to make a difference in a complex maze of competing claims and wide-ranging opportunities."[16] On the one hand are those who are lured by the power of prestige and/or wealth. Being true to the calling of their soul, which is to be a servant of love, is never considered. They perceive the sources of security to be power and wealth. Others become so determined to achieve this or that dream that they fail to consider alternatives for a more spiritually centered lifestyle. But if we do not ask, "What's my real purpose?" and if we do not consider, "What's my calling?" chances are, we will not hear God. Thus, asking fundamental questions about purpose, vocation, and meaning are crucial to the experience of holy listening.

What is the answer? Sadly, too few of us ponder the great questions of faith and meaning. Equally sad is the reality that too many of us readily claim that "Jesus is the answer" without ever thinking about exactly what it is to which he is the answer. To understand him as the answer without engaging in the question can generate a believer who spends his or her life defending a doctrinal system instead of a deepening journey of substance in Jesus as the embodiment of God's love. Such a believer's faith becomes too easily preoccupied with defending Jesus in a world that knows him not. The task of defending Jesus is energy consuming and the

---

[16] Parks, *Big Questions /Worthy Dreams*, 3.

business of judging all those who do not conform to the impression of the Jesus we feel impelled to defend leaves us little time or ability to be his love. For others, "Jesus is the answer" means an acknowledgement of Jesus but no real care or awareness of his relevance, call, and desire to impact the moment by moment decisions, thoughts, and actions of our lives, as we are called to be the incarnation of grace.

John A. T. Robinson echoes this need to understand the significance of incarnational presence when he asks, "How do we make real what the dimension of transcendence adds in this realm?"[17] In other words, if I in faith affirm that Jesus is the answer, then I cannot help but ask, "How is he the Christ for me?" Likewise, the question of "Who am I?" cannot be separated from the question of "Who is Jesus?" and the question of "What am I to do?" cannot be separated from that of, "What is Jesus doing in the world?" To grapple with such questions can revolutionize our understanding of how Jesus is the answer for our lives. Faith in him can transform our understanding of God and ourselves. Making the connection between the questions and the answer can bring about a point of commitment and a calling in life that is transforming. No longer feeling the need to defend Jesus Christ (God can pretty much take care of himself), our faith becomes oriented not around a set of beliefs but around a person. As the human face of God, he embraces us and moves us to be the incarnate face and hands and heart of God. In this way, he truly is the answer to the questions of our lives.

So what? How does the association of the questions and the answers make any impact on relationships, listening for meaning and rendering decisions in our day-to-day lives? How does this theological perspective of Jesus Christ play itself out in the ordinariness of life? Linking knowledge of self with the experience of Jesus and connecting our own pursuits with our interest in the activity of Jesus in the world means that faith's relevance is borne

---

[17] John A. T. Robinson, *The Human Face of God* (Philadelphia: The Westminster Press, 1973) 233.

out of relationships, not doctrine. Faith becomes understood and experienced as the simple ability to recognize God's "yes" amidst the clutter of our desks, as we sip coffee, as we watch the children fight and play, as we ponder the day's agenda, as we plan the budget, and as we think about the cost of maintaining a car and home and planning our retirement.[18] Every moment becomes a holy moment where time is transfused by divine love because the purposes and callings of our lives have become associated with the only answer that can satisfy the innermost longings of our hearts.

### Faith and Meaning

Sharon Daloz Parks has explored the relationship between faith and meaning from a general perspective without linking the discussion to any one particular religious construct. Her work is exemplary and one worth reading for anyone interested in understanding the relationship between faith and meaning and how we apply a healthy understanding of faith to the connections, decisions, and relationships we make in everyday life.[19] She acknowledges that for some, faith has become a matter of indifference that, if acknowledged at all, is understood as only one element of life that is often separated from discussions about career, politics, relationships, and economics. In this sense, faith is more akin to Martin Luther's vision of two kingdoms, a heavenly realm distinct from an earthly kingdom, taken to the extreme. Faith is relegated to a small segment of life, a necessary entity that looms in the background, and is only called upon in the big moments of life like births, weddings, and funerals. Such individuals believe in God and they believe in the church, but they fail to make any real connection between God's calling for their lives and the decisions they make about their lives.

At the other extreme is a notion of faith that is equated with religious dogma. Those with a dogmatic view assume they possess

---

[18] See Robert Raines's poem "Yes" in *Creative Broodings* (New York: Mac-millan Publishing Company, 1966) 114.

[19] Parks, *Big Questions/Worthy Dreams*, 14–33.

the truth. Their belief becomes static, and lines of demarcation are drawn. All who share their perspective are considered the godly, and those who hold a different perspective are viewed as the lost and the emissaries of Satan. Because adherents to dogma have lost the ability to be critical of their faith, they assure themselves of their predestined place in God's eternal kingdom, and they readily believe that they have the right to impose their perspective and experience on all others. The rigid view of many in the religious right usurps the place of God's mercy and righteousness in the divine acts of creation, judgment, and redemption. Such individuals speak in lofty terms about God's Word, but then use their own biases and preconceived judgments to impose their perspectives on others. They simply cannot fathom that others, who profess equally their belief in and devotion to Jesus Christ, come to radically different conclusions about his relevance in life and his work in society. From the standpoint of holy listening, such rigidity of faith prevents those who hold dogmatically to a particular point of view from ever changing and dogmatic practice intimidates others who seek to understand anew in order to be transformed in their faith journey.

What is one to do in making sense of faith and meaning within the confines of these two extremes? Why is it that some hold on to a very rigid faith with no willingness to change? Why is it that some have no faith at all? Why is it that still others relegate the spiritual framework to one small component of life with no bearing on career, politics, relationships, and economics? The varied responses to faith can be explained partially by how we come to know and make sense of our world. As Parks writes, "The suffering of adult faith is located in how to hold on to, and when to let go of, the perceptions, patterns, and relationships that one experiences as partaking in ultimate value and truth."[20] Because of experiences in life, some change and their faith in God becomes more complete. In the face of events and tragedies that were not planned, some hold on to and become defensive of their faith, fearing that the questions

---

[20] Parks, *Big Questions/Worthy Dreams*, 33.

that can lead to transformation are instead a slippery slope that only leads to perdition. Still others give up on any significance in God at all. In other words, life experiences, cultural contexts, and significant others all influence the way in which we draw conclusions about faith and its relevance, if any, for the world in which we live.

If faith is to have transforming meaning for the individual, then several issues are valid for consideration. Such faith will entail substantive questioning. We cannot engage in authentic conversation with God and we cannot nurture faith apart from questioning, which includes doubt. Questioning is a basic component of communication and without it, the ability to communicate and listen to God is reduced. In addition, people attempting to secure their own faith must give themselves and others the freedom to be transformed not just at the point of salvation, but throughout all of life as well. Granting such freedom involves trust not only in each other, but, more profoundly, in God. In other words, the degree to which we trust others including those with whom we differ says much about the degree to which we really trust God and the divine's ability to render the outcome of love. Finally, because suffering has such a tremendous impact on the extent to which faith is developed or rejected, the need to listen to the divine in the midst of pain and the need to hold on in the face of darkness is paramount. Engaging in holy listening means that in times of suffering, there may be the need to wait in order to arrive at awareness of the voice of God. To ponder holy listening requires that the suffering side of life be acknowledged and addressed in order to attempt to avoid shallow faith and faulty meaning. And it is to the chasm of darkness we turn in order to discern the presence of God that can only be heard on the other side of pain.

# 5

## *Listening When We Hurt*

I remember the moment vividly. As I returned home from a business trip, my wife Cheryl met me at the door. One look at her face and I knew something terribly wrong had happened. With a stare that spoke to the depth of my soul, she simply said, "I think Margaret has diabetes."

At the time, Margaret was only four years old. Neither Cheryl nor I could envision from that vantage point the enormous transition that Margaret's condition would require. The subsequent tests would confirm what Cheryl already knew. Quickly, we were ushered to the hospital where medical professionals informed us fully about diabetes, changes in lifestyle, learning how to give injections, and, even worse, how to prick Margaret's finger several times a day to maintain a reading on her blood sugar levels.

Diabetes is a frustrating chronic illness. With the disease itself, there is little control. You can manage the illness and do everything possible to prevent an insulin reaction, but you never know when a serious problem is going to occur. Emotions get out of balance. The ancient Greeks thought the disease was an emotional disorder because they observed how volatile people became when afflicted with it. Imagine having to convince your child to drink orange juice or to take glucose when they are experiencing what diabetics refer to as a "low," meaning their blood sugar levels have dropped precipitously below what is needed to sustain the body. At this point, the diabetic is convinced you are trying to attack him or her. Even worse, try administering an injection from what is known as the glucagon kit when your own child is comatose. The kit is a vile of powdered glucose and water that you must always have on hand, and it serves as a poignant reminder of what can happen at a moment's notice. Lord knows how many nights passed when Cheryl and I would worry. Margaret had a monitor in her room, and somehow we learned even in our sleep to listen to her breathing patterns. We just knew when things were not right. We would wake up and go from sleep to running down the hallway—one to Margaret's bedroom and the other to the kitchen to get the juice and the kit. Some nights we realized that Margaret was beyond the point of the juice being of aid. With hands shaking, minds pondering the worst, and hearts praying for the best, we had to mix the water and powdered glucose, administer the shot, and wait for what always seemed like a passing eternity before the ambulance arrived.

At another level, there is the reality that we live in a cosmetic culture consumed with appearances. What appears to be fine surely must be. The trouble is that diabetes has no outward symptoms, and so those unaffected never realize the emotional, physical, and financial stresses that accompany this disorder. The ordinary stresses of beginning a new school year are accompanied with the need to alert school officials that your child may have to excuse herself frequently because she needs to go to the bathroom or perhaps she needs to have a snack. Just the simple joy of going to a ballgame becomes exacerbated with the ritual of explaining to gate officials why you need to carry juice and crackers into a venue where no outside food is allowed. And then think about the added task of getting through airport security in a post-9/11 world. Injection needles, glucose monitors, and insulin pumps always arouse the curiosity of those entrusted with our security.

Diabetes also has a way of impressing finitude harshly upon a child even at an early age. Young girls love to play with dolls, dream about getting married, and think about all the other possibilities they might do with their lives. As a child, Margaret did too, but she also wondered if she would be able to have children and even worried about how long she might live and in what condition.

Margaret had a cousin who also had diabetes and who died as a young adult. As such, Margaret voiced concern along the way about what point in life she might lose one of her limbs, a kidney, or her eyes, and at what point she too might die. These are tough thoughts for a young child to ponder. Listen to her own words given in a speech to a local civic club when she was fourteen. In reflecting on her chronic illness, she said:

> I have juvenile diabetes, also known as Type I diabetes. I have had this disease since I was four years old. Just recently, I started on the insulin pump, which helps deliver insulin more like a pancreas. Before I was on the insulin pump, I had to give myself five to six shots per day. I still have to test my blood sugar up to five times a day.... My wish is that someday there will be a cure for diabetes. Even though I am on the insulin pump, I still could develop complications like blindness, kidney disease, circulatory problems and heart disease.[1]

Who can blame Margaret if she is a bit frightened and even angry at the circumstances that fate dealt her innocent life? She has accomplished much and she has done so with obstacles in her way. I am proud of her as any father would be, but I also hurt and suffer vicariously. I can only deal with the pain from the perspective of a parent, which pales in reality to the burden that she must endure each day of her life. My pain is the helplessness realized in the inability to encompass the illness in my own being. How I wish that her illness could be mine instead. My desire is the same as most parents. We want to create a context in which our children can have happy, safe, and meaningful lives. I recall feeling a sense of guilt following Margaret's diagnosis, as if somehow her physical condition was my fault. Before diabetes, I loved to make Margaret cinnamon toast. At a rational level, I knew that the cinnamon and sugar had nothing to do with the onset of diabetes. Yet I could not help but worry that in an effort to offer a gesture of love I had somehow caused the diabetes.

---

[1] Margaret Shippey, "Living with Diabetes," Cleveland Kiwanis Club, Cleveland GA, Spring 2001.

And who can blame me for being a bit angry and confused for what happened to Margaret? There have been many such moments. In anger and in doubt, I have struggled to discern how Margaret's diabetes could be the will of God. If God is a God of love, why can't human beings discover a cure for this disease? Why won't the Divine in all his power heal Margaret? Why did evil raise its ugly arm in the form of Margaret's diabetes? In moments of hurt, I have pondered such questions that address both the reality of a good and loving God and the presence of evil, including the whimsical notions of chance and fate over which I have no control, but through which evil manifests itself. The questions have been more than an intellectual exercise of theological curiosity. They have provided the context from which I have been able to listen to God in the midst of hurt.

For most of us, if you live long enough, life's finitude has a way of throwing one curve ball after another at you. Whether it is diabetes, divorce, death, or just the details of a demanding world, struggling to listen to God when we hurt becomes a real and urgent issue. How we address the suffering conditions of existence is crucial in the art of listening to God. The desire to correct what we cannot control can too easily lead to a sense of dysfunctional blame and debilitating guilt that leads to anger and deafness toward grace. But hearing the grace when we hurt is the point at which we also experience transformation in the course of time.

## The Waiting Place: Experiencing *Kairos* in the *Chronos*

Margaret's condition is an ongoing dilemma. The struggle to hear God in the midst of hurt is far more than a subject of intellectual curiosity. Cheryl and I continue to struggle to make sense of her chronic illness. There is an emptiness that we seldom acknowledge but that accompanies all we do.

I cannot speak for Margaret. I cannot speak for countless others who suffer too. All I can do is offer some word of understanding about hearing God in the midst of hurt. Experiencing God in the valley of the shadow of death is never easy and requires a diligent effort lest the pain silence the goodness of grace the divine wills to pour out in abundant measure.

Many who know pain also know of the profound opportunity to listen to God that occurs in the eye of the storm. In the vortex of the whirlpool, there is no need for excessive emotionalism, the coldness of religious legalism, or the ambivalence of spiritual relativism, which are generally the religious responses. There is need for the quiet silence of a God who in Jesus Christ knows both the anguish and the tranquility of the sufferer in the midst of raging chaos. But to arrive at such a silence that traverses through the darkness of despair is a journey in and of itself. T. S. Eliot eloquently expresses the traversing of the soul in noting that, "To arrive where you are, to get from where you are not, you must go by a way wherein there is no ecstasy."[2]

Listening when we hurt requires learning and relearning one of the most difficult lessons of all, which is the need to wait on God. Recall Sarah's laugh and the unbelieving question she asked herself saying, "After I have grown old, and my husband is old, shall I have pleasure?" (Gen 18:12, NRSV). The Lord responds to Sarah's doubt by promising, "At the set time I will return to you, in due season, and Sarah shall have a son" (Gen 18:14b, NRSV). Waiting on this "due season" is what is so difficult. We do not know the outcome and, even worse, we have little if any control over what the end result will be. But as Eliot further observes, "Only through time is time conquered."[3] Time has a way of making sense, even redeeming sense, of what we cannot grasp in the presence of the moment. Eliot's longing was for a moment in which one is released from practical desire, outer compulsion, the need to act, and the reality of suffering. His was a desire to find grace in a moment somehow suspended beyond the confines of time as past, present,

---

[2] T. S. Eliot, "East Coker," in "The Four Quartets," in *The Complete Poems and Plays: 1909–1950* (New York: Harcourt, Brace and World, Inc, 1971) 127.

[3] Eliot, "Burnt Norton," in "The Four Quartets," *The Complete Poems and Plays*, 120.

and future in which there is a knowing of exaltation "at the still point of the turning world."[4] He spoke of the need of the soul to fly like the petrel over the vast seas far from land as well as of the soul's need to find security on the shore's safe side. Eliot realized that the real beginning of meaning occurred not so much in the casual moments of our lives but rather in the possibility of transformation that occurs when finitude and destiny meet, giving birth to new insight, understanding, purpose, and calling. As he writes:

> Love is most nearly itself
> When here and now cease to matter....
> Here and there does not matter
> We must be still and still moving
> Into another intensity
> For a further union, a deeper communion
> Through the dark cold and the empty desolation,
> The wave cry, the wind cry, the vast waters
> Of the petrel and the porpoise. In my end is my beginning.[5]

The end that is the beginning in a biblical way of thinking is a concept of time known as the gift of *kairos*. This is the concept of time in which the eternal breaks into the temporal or the *chronos* of our ordinary lives. *Kairos* is time that is pregnant with new understanding. Crucial for learning to listen to God when we hurt is the need to be open to the moment of *kairos* during which the in-breaking of God gives meaning to *chronos* by providing us hope, sustaining us with love, and transforming us through faith. In acknowledging the confession of the writer of Ecclesiastes that "all is vanity," Paul Tillich observed that faith allows one to move beyond a sense of the futility of life.[6] Faith opens one to an

---

[4] Ibid., 119.

[5] Eliot, "East Coker," in "The Four Quartets," *The Complete Poems and Plays*, 129.

[6] Paul Tillich, "The Right Time," in *The New Being* (New York: Charles Scribner's Sons, 1955) 161–69. See also Paul Tillich, *Systematic*

awareness of time that sees life as a vessel of God's eternity instead of a sequence of the mundane measured by the passing of the clock from one moment to the next. Even in those contexts where we hurt so profoundly that our lungs are full of grief, the moment of *kairos* seeks to encompass those who are open to the Incarnation's love. Opening oneself to this love, however, requires that one open oneself to the divine rest and the depth of its quiet. This place of quiet rest is the seedbed in the midst of the noise of existence from which transformation occurs that does not bypass the tragedy so common to *chronos*, but embraces it in the reality of the cross that is the heart of God and his love.[7]

## The God who Suffers with Us

Our age is replete with suffering. From the AIDS crisis in Africa to fighting in the Middle East to homelessness in the United States, common to our reality is suffering. People hurt. They endure pain. They die.

In addition, ours is a time of instability. It used to be that you could count on the corporation to provide employment for life. Now, corporations, forced by changing economics, provide little security. The Protestant work ethic and its promise of stability and reward in exchange for hard work is now called into question. Common to our time is the reality that people are insecure.

One explanation in the Old Testament, which parenthetically highlights how faith in the Bible evolves, was the concept of reward/retribution theology. Do well and you will prosper. Do not, and God will punish you. This harshness in the Old Testament point of view is most evident in the book of Job, as detailed in the conversations between Job and his friends. You may recall that Job lost everything he owned and every person he loved. Job insisted that he had done nothing to deserve the punishment he received.

---

*Theology: Three Volumes in One* (Chicago: The University of Chicago Press, 1967) 3:369–372.

[7] See Paul Tillich, "The Yoke of Religion," in *The Shaking of the Foundations*, (New York: Charles Scribner's Sons, 1976) 102–103.

Having all that he owned and all that was dear taken from him, Job knew in his heart that he was innocent. But his friends responded with the conventional religious wisdom of the day. Job must have surely sinned or else God would not be punishing him. In the end, his plight is resolved in the infinite mystery of God. But the book represents a hallmark in thinking and initiates the transition away from an understanding of God as harsh toward an understanding of the Divine as One whose righteousness is his mercy. The book also reminds us that while it is true that there are consequences to poor judgment and that these consequences can wreak devastating effects on our world and in our lives, the reality is also true, to which Job attested, that the innocent do suffer.

There is no clearer testimony in the Bible that the innocent suffer than the agony of Jesus on Good Friday. At a minimum, this saga is a testimony to one's faithfulness to God even amidst the restlessness of life's tumultuous seas. Looking at Good Friday, a profound question emerges. How does the humiliation of Jesus on the cross have any meaning or provide any hope to those who suffer? I am reminded of a story that Dennis Turner, a former pastor of mine, used to tell about an experience his mother had as a teacher. Mrs. Turner happened to notice a young child who had lost both of his parents at an early age sitting on a bench during recess. One parent had died from an extended illness and the other as a result of a car accident. The teacher observed that the child, sitting all alone, was quietly crying. She asked, "Are you alright?" The young child responded, "I miss my parents so much." Following recess, Mrs. Turner told the story to some of her fellow teachers. One asked, "What did you do?" She said, "I did the only thing I could do. I sat in silence and embraced the child." Similarly, the cross of Jesus Christ is God's embrace of each of us in the totality of our hurt, failure, and sin.

The power of God is such that the Divine is most readily recognized in the willingness of Jesus Christ to suffer and die for the sake of humanity. This means that Jesus Christ radically alters the Christian's view of God. His lordship is understood not in terms of immutability or omnipotence—those classic doctrines that speak to the unchanging, all-powerful nature of God—but rather in the Divine's infinite capacity to serve. What is unchanging about the nature of God that Jesus Christ reveals is the Divine's infinite capacity to love. Instead of speaking about God's omnipotence or immutability, Karl Barth preferred to speak of the constancy of God and observed:

> God is immutably the One whose reality is seen in His conde-scension in Jesus Christ, in His self-offering and self-concealment, in His self-emptying and self-humiliation. He is not a God who is what He is in a majesty behind the condescension, behind the cross on Golgotha. On the contrary, the cross on Golgotha is itself the divine majesty...[which reveals] that God on high is the One who was able and willing and in fact did condescend so completely to us in His Son. This free love is the one true God Himself.[8]

This is the kind of God with whom we have to listen and in whom we have hope even as we suffer. Recall the previous discussion on the *Abba* experience of God and Phillips's observation that the Divine does not sit as a "grand old man" who judges like a sage from a distance far removed from the realities of our world.[9] Rather, the Divine is present in the form of One who is constant love, having revealed in Jesus Christ the depths to which he is willing to go in order to embrace each of us. The true God is revealed in the humiliation of the cross. There is no point of suffering and no vestige of death that God does not feel or encompass. This reality speaks to the heart of waiting and to the time of uncertainty in ways that remind the innocent that they are not alone. While at times we know not where the door of light is, let alone how to walk through it, there is abiding love that accompanies the wounded believer. Listening to this love is the faithful invitation of the Gospel.

---

[8] Karl Barth, *Church Dogmatics*, ed. and trans. G. W. Bromiley and T. F. Torrance (Edinburgh: T. & T. Clark, 1961) vol. 2, pt. 1, 517.

[9] J. B. Phillips, *Your God is Too Small* (New York: A Touchstone Book, 1997) 23–26.

## On the Other Side of Pain

In a world full of pain, suffering, and tragic death, how can one hear God? There is no adequate explanation for suffering. Whatever word is rendered never adequately resolves the question of why the innocent suffer. Such discourse most always pales in the face of the suffering itself. In other words, at its most personal level, I can never offer an explanation that will satisfy Margaret's condition. All I or any theologian or philosopher can do is offer a word of hope grounded in the faith of what one believes God to be like and how one understands God to be working even in the depths of hurt and despair.

And at some level, there is even selfishness in focusing on Margaret's suffering, as her condition is symptomatic of the larger reality of fate's harsh judgment on all of us. But her condition has shaped my thinking about why innocent people suffer and has reinforced my faith in the unchanging nature of God's constant love. What follows is a brief theodicy, or attempt to explain how a good and loving God works in a world of evil to bring about the Divine's redemptive end, which is the consummation of the Kingdom of God.

Perhaps the classic portrayal of suffering in the twentieth century can be found in Picasso's *Guernica*. The stark mural portrays the bleakness of life in war-ravaged Spain during Germany's invasion prior to World War II. Both the Italian and German Air Forces bombed the Basque village of Guernica in what was the first exercise in saturated bombing that resulted in the deaths of over 1,000 people. The painting is seen as accurately portraying what Paul Tillich has described as the "disruptiveness, existential doubt, emptiness and meaninglessness" so common to our time.[10] In *Guernica*, Picasso grotesquely portrays the reality of suffering, seemingly silencing any word of redemptive hope from an all-powerful God.

---

[10] Paul Tillich, *Christianity and the Existentialists*, ed. Carl Michalson (New York: Charles Scribner's Sons, 1956) 138.

Pablo Picasso, *Guernica*; 1937 (Museo del Prado, Madrid)

Picasso once observed, "Art is a lie that makes us realize the truth."[11] His intent in *Guernica* was to make a political statement about the injustice of the bombing and the horror of war. But the painting is striking in a spiritual context as well, and given the art of listening, perhaps one has to see the "lie" of reality and its destructive consequences before one can hear God. Observe the light at the top of the picture. Some have interpreted this as the eye of God's judgment. But in Spanish, an electric bulb or lamp is called "bombilla," which is suggestive of the saturated bombing and the subsequent suffering and death caused not by the judgment of God, but rather of humanity against humanity. Perhaps Picasso was lamenting the lethal power of technology and its capacity to destroy. One cannot help but wonder where God is in the sea of death portrayed by decapitated heads, severed arms, dying children, and wailing women.

---

[11] Robert Cumming, *Art: The World's Greatest Paintings Explored and Explained* (London: ADK Publishing Book, 1995) 98.

I suggest that the presence of God is found both as judgment and as hope in this painting. Judgment is conveyed in the piercing eye of the bull whose body lost (sacrificial image) now sits in quiet condemnation over the stage of death created by the injustice of humankind. The kind of world in which God chose to operate is a world where human beings are free to create good or ill. The judgment is the consequence that humanity poses on itself for creating a hell on earth. The bull's piercing eye evokes the lament of God overseeing the cold, cruel reality that humanity has chosen for itself. But as is the case for any true prophet, Picasso does not only render the bad news. The mural includes a glimmer of hope for a tomorrow that might emerge from the depiction of this day's death. That hope lies in the small fragile presence of a flower rising from the ashes of destruction.

The mural is preceded by the 1930 painting *La Crucifixion*, which depicts Picasso's understanding of the pain of the crucifixion and the horror of death induced by asphyxiation. There is stark similarity between the ghastly impression of the dying Christ in *La Crucifixion* and the wounded horse in *Guernica*, both of which are central focal points in the respective paintings. Picasso, loathe to interpret his own paintings, once acknowledged that the wounded horse was a symbol of hurting people. The cold stone figure draped on a cross amid a sea of color suggests awareness of Christ's presence in the center of forces of raging chaos. When the two paintings are viewed together, a critical insight emerges concerning listening to God when we hurt. Before art can depict beauty, it must, as Thompson observes, "make the detour through struggling with evil before finding a central reservoir of meaning in human existence."[12] Central to faith is the necessity of realizing the presence of God in the reality of suffering so common to life. Just as doubt and questioning can lead to a more meaningful, mature faith, so too one must often struggle in the wilderness before seeing the

---

[12] William M. Thompson, *The Jesus Debate: A Survey & Synthesis* (New York: Paulist Press, 1985) 27–29.

flower of hope or hearing the presence of God's love in the chaos of our lives.

Pablo Picasso, *La Crucifixion*; 1930 (Musée Picasso, Paris)

Picasso's brilliant works capture this central truth by immersing the viewer in the horror of Nothingness and its atmosphere of demonic darkness while yet holding out hope for tomorrow as portrayed in the presence of a fragile flower. While one cannot know what Picasso thought concerning the empathy and activity of a loving God, the similarity of the two paintings certainly leaves the impression that Picasso was keenly aware in his own life that at a minimum Christ represented the attestation of a God willing to embrace pain. The flower in *Guernica* is for me the promise of God's love and remains a symbol of hope that can be found for the discerning soul in the havoc of our lives. Looking for this flower that can only be found in the midst of the decay is an opportunity to hear the presence of the good and loving God that is felt most keenly on the other side of pain. In the midst of hurt and fear where fate has willed its random claim on our lives, there is the occasion to experience grace in a new day's dawning, if we will but look and listen.

But how? *Guernica* provides a backdrop of darkness from which the sea of suffering and death emerges and to which hope and faith must respond. Picasso's painting is reminiscent of Karl Barth's description of Nothingness that was quite similar to the bleak darkness that gives rise to the graphic pain depicted in *Guernica*. Barth perceived that evil emerges from a realm of Nothingness that seeks to siege God's declaration of creation as good.[13] Barth understood creation as the Divine's pronouncement of a "yes" to all that is good. But just as a state or a nation has a boundary and borders by which to identify itself, Barth reasoned that there was a boarder region in which creation resided. That which was outside the border Barth believed to be the legitimate "no" of existence, which represented the shadow side of creation. From this realm, Barth realized that limitation, decay, suffering, and death were a part of the natural order. To be sure, at a personal level suffering is real, but nonetheless a natural part of life. The sun rises and it must set. But within this shadow side emerged the real threat to existence, which is the demonic element of evil that not only threatens creation, but seeks to threaten God as well. Barth referred to this reality as Nothingness. The existence of Nothingness is the source from which evil and its ensuing realm of sin and fate arise.

Fate's reality should not be minimized, as it is the powerful arm of Nothingness that holds random sway over all of us. At a personal level, this means that Margaret has diabetes and another child has cancer because of the reality of fate. Each condition is not

---

[13] Barth, *Church Dogmatics*, vol. 3, pt. 3, 296–97.

the result of a capricious God who judges, punishes, and condemns one for sin. And while the realities of such innocent suffering can build character, God does not impose suffering on people in order to make one strong in faith. I would not harm my children in order to help them develop a character of perseverance. If my conscience does not allow me to implement such a harsh measure, neither does a good and loving God engage in the business of willing hurt on people in order to help them eternally. I cannot see the suffering of Margaret or any countless number of human beings over our long history as the result of a predetermined fixed will of God carrying out some mysterious plan that includes his intention that each of us suffer. L. D. Johnson struggles with the power of fate and its seemingly uncontrollable nature and ponders how one can make sense of a good and loving God in the midst of the tragedies that mark our existence. He reflects about the death of his own daughter, Carol, through a tragic automobile accident and writes, "If God is God, could he not have kept the accident from happening? The slight alteration of any one of several contingencies would have produced another result. One twist of the wheel, a hundred yards ahead or behind on the road—a tiny significant detail—ten ticks of her little Swiss watch—and she would have missed the truck that crushed out her life....Why didn't God intervene?"[14]

Johnson goes on to reject explanations about evil that include the Divine's decision to distance himself from the world, thereby leaving the world to its own chaotic devices. He rejects the view that God has predetermined everything and that all that happens is a result of God's order or decree. Johnson also refutes the perspective that life is just a game of chance that has no divine direction, and he cannot accept the belief that pain and evil are just illusions of the mind. He concludes that there is no adequate

---

[14] L. D. Johnson, *The Morning after Death* (Nashville: Broadman Press, 1978) 101.

explanation. In faith, he trusts that there is for the Christian only an answer, which is Jesus Christ.[15]

Fate's reality is the result of all that threatens the grace of God. Fate is an intrusion from the realm of Nothingness that invades all that God wills for each life. I do not mean to imply that fate itself has a predetermined set of objectives. Too often, fatalism's response is a cold resignation expressed in terms of "my number's up" or in the assumption that "whatever will be, will be." If Christ is the answer, then faith's response is that grace itself has become the victim and the judgment in order to be the light of love. As Frank Tupper writes, "The God of grace is the primary victim and the relentless enemy of Nothingness.... The God of grace became one with us, a threatened, ruined, and lost creature to judge and destroy Nothingness."[16]

Even so, fate remains the expressive arm of evil that seeks at random to impose its will upon us. To be sure, such a perspective acquiesces to fate a reality in which even God has self-limited the Divine's complete control. In the kind of free world that God chose to create, the ability of fate to express itself from the dark realm of Nothingness is real. Fate itself is an element that God allows to exist. Why the Divine does so is a question I can only contemplate. In other words, if God is truly God, why doesn't he end the ugly shadow of Nothingness and its accompanying fate? Against the demands of this perplexing question, the story of Jesus Christ is an invitation to trust in the Divine's love, believing that its power will ultimately rule over the threat of fate. In this free world, God has willed that human beings freely come to him. The whole history of providence is the working of God with creation to bring about the ultimate and definitive "yes" that will subdue and destroy fate's imposition upon all that is good. In this sense, God is involved in a game of chess where fate makes its claim upon us and God responds

---

[15] Ibid., 102–17. See also E. Frank Tupper's commentary on L. D. Johnson's perspective in *A Scandalous Providence: The Jesus Story of the Compassionate God* (Macon: Mercer University Press, 1995) 208–11.

[16] Tupper, *Scandalous*, 142.

redemptively and always with the certainty of his kingdom's end. God reigns always with the intentional end of his redemptive purpose, which is the ability to respond with the aim of love even in the face of evil's onslaught. Was the risk of creation worth the intrusion of fate and its ensuing suffering that is so common to existence? I think it far better to have Margaret with diabetes than to not have Margaret at all. Her presence itself is God's gift of grace. And for any of us who hurt, being able to see the grace borne out of the intensity of the pain is necessary if we are to hear the God who knows the depth of despair in the cross and who works for our hope in the resurrection.

Between the tensions of the cross and the resurrection, between defeat and exaltation, between God's death in the Son and his life in exaltation, between utter absence and complete presence, between silence and miracle, and between defeat and hope is the place where we hear God in our hurt. We live in a world that God created in which he also chose to limit his involvement. He did this to render the possibility that we might freely choose his love for our lives. Not always involved at the point of altering a sequence of events immersed in *chronos* time, God nonetheless is forever present. We live in a world where God's miracle in the specific moment does not always happen but also in a world that has been shaped by the ultimate miracle of all, which is that God came as flesh and dwelt among us.

In Margaret's case, I wonder why God does not intervene. Beyond her need, I wonder why God does not prevent fate from wreaking disaster. What word can I offer Margaret? What word can I offer myself? I do believe that the Divine is immersed in the details of the suffering, silently weeping with Margaret and me in our human grief. I also believe that God is eschatologically working in the moment to redeem the suffering for eternity. Put another way, the cross is the place where God weeps with us and loves us in our own despair. A mistake is made when we too quickly move to the resurrection and its glory, which is only so because of the depth of darkness revealed in the death of Jesus on the cross. Golgotha is the place where God weeps. Golgotha is too the place where God weeps for Margaret and each of us in the face of all that hurts and over which we have no control.

Moving from the pain of Golgotha and its cold darkness, I am left with bitterness or the need for hope. In the final analysis, the word offered is one of trust in the hope that is God's love received through the desolation of the cross. Only after we let the cross embrace us is there need to look at life from the perspective of the resurrection. In the resurrection, we can let go of our hurting and give it to the promise that God's love is the final word. Love, God's love, moves toward each of us and sustains us in the middle of all that we cannot understand. His "yes" is the final word, which is love. In this love, the questions of time will be resolved in the answer of Jesus Christ. As the poet Rilke expressed it, "Be patient toward all that is unresolved in your heart and try to love the questions themselves.... Live the questions now. Perhaps you will then gradually, without noticing it, live along some distant day into the answer."[17] Hearing the "yes," borne in the cross and confirmed in the hope of the resurrection, has been essential in my awareness of the engaging presence of God in the chaos of pain, suffering, and vestiges of death.

What does this conviction concerning God's presence mean for an understanding of the possibilities for hearing God when we hurt? Central to faith in Jesus Christ is the certitude that in the face of suffering, whatever its cause and regardless of its origin, God takes the suffering into his inner-most being. This is the meaning of the teaching that "God so loved the world that He gave His only Son" (John 3:16, NRSV). The Divine addresses human suffering, sin, and death by Jesus Christ's willingness, as Barth writes, "to suffer the wrath of God in His own body and the fire of His love in His own soul."[18] The cross is the clearest revelation of the eternal nature of God. In the silence of the cross, the voice of hope speaks about the coming gift of resurrection. If this is true, then there is

---

[17] Rainer Maria Rilke, *Letters to a Young Poet*, trans. M. D. Herter Norton (New York: Norton, 1993) 35.

[18] Barth, *Church Dogmatics*, vol. 4, pt. 1, 93–96.

hope in the possibility of listening to God in the face of grief, pain, disappointment, suffering, helplessness, alienation, despair, and the ever-looming presence of death. Why? Because in this darkness there is God. He speaks with a heart of love that Barth referred to as "omnipotent mercy." Of this God, Barth further observed: "Love for Him is love for the Crucified. Hope in Him is hope in the Crucified.... We have not seen the Jesus of the Gospels and the whole of the New Testament properly if we do not finally take account of the fact that the light in which we have tried to see Him is the light of His death as it shines forth in His resurrection, and that it is in this way that it is the light of His life, the light of the world."[19]

The particularity of this light and of this love speaks to the heart of fate's randomness. In Jesus Christ, the response to fate is not the cold, scientific rationalization of natural selection, but rather the emerging and evolving awareness of God's love. Related to this emphasis on the awareness of divine love is a needed corrective to the doctrine of atonement, which seeks to explain how the death of Jesus Christ reconciled humanity to God. The doctrine of atonement has historically been explained in part as a transaction where the death of Jesus either satisfied a ransom to Satan or somehow appeased or satisfied God. The result was the redemption of humanity. But such a notion of atonement really cheapens the nature of God and is a misrepresentation of the act of the cross. Atonement is God's willingness to be at one with humanity in the only way possible for costly redemption and grace to be manifest. Atonement is ultimately a testimony to the willingness of God to journey into the randomness of our realm in order to redeem intentionally. The incarnational act of the Divine in the atonement is who God has chosen to be. This is his love. Against all suffering that cannot be explained fully and amidst all that cannot be understood definitively, the face of Jesus as the Christ is the face of love that renders hope and meaning even in despair.

---

[19] Barth, *Church Dogmatics*, vol. 4, pt. 2, 250.

This point was brought home during my years of doctoral study. My major written assignment was an analysis of the meaning of the suffering of God—a heavy subject to be sure. As is true with most students in seminary, I had a family for which I was responsible, a demanding administrative job, and the relentless task of completing a dissertation the end of which I thought would never come. Far into the task, I recall feeling as low emotionally as I had ever felt in my life. Exhausted and feeling poor, frustrated, and uncertain, the intellectual concept of analyzing the suffering of God gave way to a vexing of my own soul. At a critical point in the research, I discovered a wonderful book about the life of Mozart.[20] The question I was pondering was "if God has acted once-and-for-all in Jesus Christ, why is it that I feel so thirsty for his living water?"

The plaguing reality of Nothingness and the emergence of suffering had numbed my ability to sense joy, laughter, and play in life. The book marveled at Mozart's sense of peace in the aftermath of the Lisbon earthquake that occurred in the latter half of the eighteenth century. Evidence of his peace was his ability to write in this tumultuous period a very playful tune titled "The Magic Flute." He wrote from a "mysterious center," as Barth described it, that allowed "the rays of the sun to drive out the night."[21] Mozart's gift was his ability to realize that in life, there is both light and darkness. He saw that just as it is true that there is darkness that always accompanies light, equally true is the fact that in darkness there is also light. Just as there is joy that is accompanied by sorrow, so too is the reality that even in the midst of sorrow there is also joy. This insight provided a major turning point in my analysis of the redemptive hope of God's suffering and provided me with a life lesson that has been so helpful as my family has struggled at times with Margaret's diabetes. Picasso's inclusion of the flower in *Guernica* conveys this same truth in which the discerning heart can

---

[20] Karl Barth, *Wolfgang Amadeus Mozart*, trans. Clarence K. Pott (Grand Rapids: William B. Eerdmans Publishing Company, 1986).

[21] Ibid., 102–103.

open even in the awareness of great suffering. From a Christian faith perspective, in the midst of suffering, Jesus Christ is the source of joy. In reflecting on Mozart, Barth observed Jesus Christ is the "yes" that is always louder than the ever-present "no." As the Heidelberg Catechism professes, "In the greatest trials I have the assurance that by His unutterable anguish, pain and terror which he suffered even in soul both on and before the cross, my Lord Christ has redeemed me from the fear and pain of hell."[22]

What then can one say in the face of pain? My experience with Margaret has drawn the conclusion that I either choose to listen in hope or choose to deafen my soul in anger, guilt, and blame. I choose to hear hope in the midst of pain or I choose to let the pain deafen the possibility for hope. I choose despair or I choose the joy of God's love, which is my hope.

Experiencing God in a world where fate works to assault all that is godly means that sometimes life will be a sojourn in a wilderness. Life's finitude makes us vulnerable to the threat of fate. Things just happen that cause inexplicable suffering that are not in the will of God. But listening to God when we hurt holds out for the possibility of hearing God in the silence of suffering. Amid the vicissitudes of life, there is a conscious choice available wherein one is open to the grace of life that gives air to breathe, a community to sustain, and strength to persevere. Epictetus, the Greek philosopher, once observed that it is the wise soul "who does not grieve for the things which he has not, but rejoices for that which he has." Listening to God is simply being mindful that life itself is a gift to be cherished, that there are people to love, and that the secret of life's meaning, even in pain, is to be consumed with the desire to look for the best in others and to give them the best that we have. In doing so, I consciously choose to trust the love of God revealed on the cross and confirmed in the coming fullness of the Divine's Kingdom of agape love. In the darkness of the "no" that assaults me, I cling to the "yes" that God loves me and is directing all that I am and feel into his heart and his care.

---

[22] Barth, *Church Dogmatics*, vol. 4, pt. 2, 605.

The alternative, it seems to me, is a hell to which we condemn ourselves by refusing to open our hearts to the Divine who wills to give us peace. C. S. Lewis wrote, "To enter heaven is to become more human than you ever succeeded in being in earth; to enter hell is to be banished from humanity."[23] The observation, I would suggest, is equally true in the here and now. To dwell in the far country of the Prodigal Son and to refuse to return home because of ignorance, pride, stubbornness, guilt, hate, or anger is the journey of isolation from oneself, one's neighbor, and God. The isolation brought on by this choice is the dehumanization of life that is hell (Luke 15:11–31). But to listen for the sound of the flute and to look for the beauty of the flower, especially in the moment of sorrow, is to become more human and, therefore, more like the image of God. To listen in such times is to hear the presence of the Paraclete, Comforter, and the indwelling Presence of God who intersects our time with transforming love (John 14:15–21). To listen in the silence is to wait for the coming presence of the Lord who does not forsake the faithful but sojourns with them, holding out for the promise of the fullness of his kingdom, which scripture points to as the final decree of God already accomplished in his time but not yet realized in ours.

## The Christian Hope

When one speaks of hope in a biblical context, most often the hope centers on that which is to come. The prayer is for a new heaven and a new earth. There is longing for eternal fellowship with God. Jürgen Moltmann is particularly helpful in articulating a sense of faith in the future eschatological hope that is grounded in the particularity of Jesus Christ.[24] To understand the future love of God's kingdom, one need look no further than the love revealed in the life, death, and resurrection of Jesus Christ. His life and death

---

[23] C. S. Lewis, *The Problem of Pain* (New York: Macmillan Publishing Company, 1962) 125.

[24] Jürgen Moltmann, *Theology of Hope*, trans. James W. Leitch (London: SCM Press, 1967) 216–24.

embody God's willingness to embrace the suffering of our own lives. But his resurrection confirms the dawning of a new creation in which not only Jesus as Lord but all who follow are exalted to fellowship with God. This exaltation is God's promise grounded in the past and delivered from the future that is the hope of every believer. And this promise of hope in Christ, therefore, has meaning for the here and now.

Christian hope is not the same as the everyday kinds of hope that we look to for satisfaction and pleasure. Being disappointed because I did not win the lottery is a mundane hope. Such peripheral hope is completely alien to the Christian hope that is always directed toward the Divine and is the driving principle that generates a sense of spiritual depth and destiny. Christian hope is rooted in God's love and rests solely in Jesus Christ. It is a hope rooted not in some utopia where pain does not exist, but rather a hope borne in pain and driven by a sense of our destiny in God.

The book of Romans is a marvelous analysis of how Jesus Christ takes on the conditions of human existence including our sins and failures, thereby justifying and making us whole before God (Rom 3:21–26). This justification has its full impact in the promise of God's glorious future where nothing will separate us from the love of God (Rom 8:39). But this future hope has meaning for the present. Paul speaks of a peace that is not absent of conflict but full of hope because of the love of God poured out in Jesus Christ and sustained now through the presence of the Holy Spirit (Rom 5:1–11). Paul understands life on the one hand as a prison in which we all live condemned by the life of Adam. On the other hand, Paul points to freedom and peace made possible through the life of Jesus Christ (Rom 5:12–21). The refrain is echoed in 1 Corinthians 15:22 where Paul writes, "For as in Adam all die, so also in Christ shall all be made alive" (RSV). While the hope to which Paul speaks no doubt has an emphasis on the eschatological future, the importance of this hope for the present and the peace that Christ now affords must also be emphasized (Rom 5:17).

In the analysis of hope that Paul provides, one can discern a crescendo that leads to the affirmation that neither "height, nor depth, nor anything else in all creation, will be able to separate us from the love of God in Christ Jesus our Lord" (Rom 8:39, NRSV). The Living New Testament paraphrases this by referring to height as "high above the sky" and depth as "the deepest ocean" and testifies that "hell itself cannot keep God's love away" (Rom 8:38–39, LNT). The affirmation is grounded in the context of the present where divine wrath, human sin, the law, and even death result from Adam's imprisonment upon us (Rom 5–8). Unfortunately, the church has immersed itself in discussions about original sin and how sin is inherited, obscuring the most basic point that Paul seeks to make, which is that sin is personal and its consequences are real (Rom 1:18–32). Through Christ, Paul believes that the opportunity exists for each person no longer to be a slave of sin but rather a slave of God, which is Paul's way of saying true freedom occurs when one moves to the point of being totally dependent upon the Divine. In this way, there is freedom from sin, freedom from the law, and freedom from death so that we become alive in the Spirit (Rom 8:1–11). This is the Christian hope for the "not yet" to be realized in God's future but also for the "already" made possible in Jesus Christ.

Does Paul's perspective on hope have any real merit for those of us who suffer, who fail, who hurt, and who feel alone in a prism of chaos? The Christian hope of which Paul speaks is rooted in absolute dependence upon God in whom reconciliation is the response to wrath (Rom 5), being made whole is the response to sin (Rom 6), liberation is the response to the law (Rom 7), and adoption as God's own is the response to death (Rom 8). After Paul acknowledges the peace that God gives through faith in Jesus Christ, he speaks of the hope that will not disappoint, realized through suffering, endurance, and increased character. This suffering is what God wills, but faith takes suffering and trusts God in its midst to produce endurance and character. In such moments, faith listens to the grace of the One who speaks from the depth of our isolation and pain. Our hope is the gift of God's love that is poured out for those who live with confidence in the face of all that leads to death because they experience the God that lives within them (Rom 5:1–5).

C. H. Dodd observed that Paul's teaching is one you either disbelieve or recognize as the Word of God.[25] Some days I believe this is God's Word. Some days I forget and even doubt. Some days Paul's words are just theoretical gibberish. But some days they remind me that life need not be managed by the fear that seeks to consume and the anger that wants to destroy. Fear and anger are destructive realities that lead to hate and seek to separate each of us from our neighbor and from all that matters in life. Paul's word, God's Word, also reminds me that listening in the silence of suffering can open me to an awareness of God that is stronger than fear and to a redemption that overcomes the anger induced by the sense of failure and alienation in life over all that I cannot control.

From the Christian point of view, what else really can any of us say in the face of all that we cannot understand or manage? In our sufferings, either we go it alone, becoming the center and lord of our own destiny, or we acknowledge a different way embodied in the life of Jesus Christ. In the silence, his Spirit speaks, yearning to remind us that we are loved—not so much because we are really worth loving—but because that is just who he is: Love.

Given the choice of facing fate and all its perils alone or facing life with the light of love, I in faith listen to the One who has taken on the depth of death's finitude and despair in order to offer hope. I need Jesus, and I am grateful for is his costly love. Moreover, I remain dependent upon his grace, which is the sound of "The Magic Flute," the beauty of the small, fragile flower of *Guernica*, and the context of countless other expressions of joy that emerge from the darkness as an altar of light speaking directly to my

---

[25] Peter Rhea Jones, "Preaching from Romans" in *Review and Expositor* 3/4 (Fall 1976): 474.

failures, doubts, and hurts reminding me that from the humus borne of decay is the seedbed for new life.

# 6

## Listening toward Light

The first time I recall encountering silence as a part of worship was at a local meeting of the Society of Friends in a Quaker Meeting House in Louisville, Kentucky. Winters in Louisville are not much fun. The wind rips off the Ohio River, and its chill can cut right through you. On such a cold morning, I decided to go to the Meeting House. Talk about an alternative form of worship! I was used to being in Baptist churches where the emphasis was on constant stimulation. Engaging in silence was something new to me. I remember sitting on the cold, hard wooden bench for what seemed like an eternity. My sole task was to sit in silence, to think of my own journey with God, the needs of others, loved ones, and to wait on a stirring of God's Spirit. The silence made an impression. That Quaker morning has left me thinking now for more years than I care to admit about the value of silence in opening us to a new awareness of the presence of God.

In recent years, while traveling through Asia, I was reminded again of the need to cultivate silence at a Buddhist monastery in Chiang Mai, Thailand. A Buddhist monk with whom I was speaking talked to me about the art of breathing. He observed that we all take breathing for granted and yet air is the "life force" necessary for existence. His point was that it is odd that we so often overlook one of the necessities for life. To focus on breathing was for him to focus on the meaning of living. Being aware of the tiniest sensations that include the rising and falling of the muscles in the abdomen and even the tickling of the nostrils as the air is taken in and released helped him gain a sense of perspective about what really mattered in terms of his thinking, emotions, aspirations, speech, behavior, and purpose. As he talked, I could not help but apply the concept to the Christian awareness of the Holy Spirit. If breath is that which sustains us physically, even more so is the need to be aware of God. Just as the monk practiced the art of breathing in order to meditate on the meaning of his own journey toward truth, there is need for each of us to meditate intentionally on the presence of God in the solitude of silence in order to hear the divine in the confusion of our loud world.

Richard Foster's, *Celebration of Discipline* is one of the great books on spiritual meditation.[1] Foster clearly portrays the inward and outward disciplines necessary for one to develop the practice of meditation as a way of life. He observes that the major prerequisite for learning is longing for God.[2] What is essential for meditation is not so much the methodology employed but the attitude that desires to seek God's presence in the daily routine of living. Foster does caution the reader not to view mediation strictly as an Eastern art. Moreover, he distinguishes the Christian forms of meditation that focus on "filling the mind" from those of the East that focus on, in his words, "emptying the mind," but this criticism is a bit harsh. The recognition in the East is that you cannot fill the mind with the presence of light until you have first emptied the mind of its desires, which lead to sadness and destruction. The Eastern position is in fact quite similar to Foster's own thinking when he writes, "Without silence, there is no solitude."[3] The reality is that you cannot listen until you have first emptied your mind and heart of the chaos of life.

In addition to emptying the mind, there is also the need to equip ourselves with some method or practice through which we can intentionally focus on God. Jesus told us not to be anxious. He

---

[1] Richard J. Foster, *Celebration of Discipline: The Path to Spiritual Growth*, rev. ed. (San Francisco: HarperSanFrancisio, 1988).

[2] Ibid., 2.

[3] Ibid., 98.

told us that we were blessed when we recognize how poor we are spiritually apart from God. He promised God's comfort to those who genuinely mourn for the welfare of others. He laid out the expectation of a steadfast commitment and focus in life. He called people to long for righteousness and to be mercy, purity, and peace (Matt 5:3–12). He taught us how to pray and how to fast (Matt 6:1–18), and he reminded us to build houses on rock and not on sand (Matt 7:24–27). But Jesus left little by way of instruction concerning steps to take or a plan to follow in order to address the difficulties and chaos that keep us from listening to God in a loud world.

But the biblical witness is clear that the essence of human existence is total and complete dependency on God's grace. The willingness to sojourn in silence is the place where we can begin to listen for this grace, which is the transforming light and presence of God. Listening toward this divine light is the necessary centering of the soul in God, and holy listening requires an acknowledgement of our brokenness apart from the Divine. Such listening also requires a silencing of the selfishness of our own lives. As Sid Wooten, one of my dear friends, who became deaf as an adult, once wrote to me, "It is indeed a loud world. I know that now because it is quiet in my world. When the noise goes away one must honestly face the reality of what life is all about."[4] Thomas Merton beautifully expresses this sense of silence that comes only in brokenness over against the loud confusion of our world in his prayer for solitude. Merton prays:

> In solitude I have at last discovered that You desire the love of my heart, O my God, the love of my heart as it is—the love of my human heart. I have found and have known by Your great mercy that the love of a heart that is abandoned and broken and poor is most pleasing to You and attracts the gaze of Your pity. It is Your desire and Your consolation, O my Lord, to be very close to those who love You and call upon You as their Father. You have perhaps no greater *consolation* (sic.)—If I may so speak—than to console Your afflicted children and those who come to You poor and empty

---

[4] Sid Wooten, e-mail message to author, 14 August 2003.

handed, with nothing but their humanness, their limitations and their great trust in Your mercy.[5]

The guiding image for listening born of an awareness of our complete humanness and total trust can be seen in Michelangelo's, *Creation of Adam*, which is in the Vatican's Sistine Chapel. Beautifully portrayed is the hand of God reaching out for the hand of humankind. The infinite space that separates the two hands reaching for each other both intrigues and disturbs me. This space, ever so small and yet ever so large, is the place of silence that must be embraced if indeed the hand of the Divine is to touch the heart of humankind. This space represents the silence that is both the invitation for divine nearness and the occasion for human separation from God.

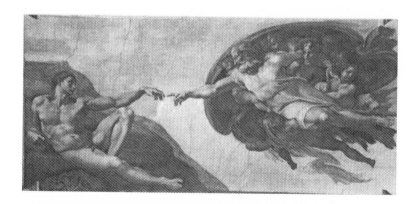

Michelangelo's, *Creation of Adam*; 1508–1512
(The Sistine Chapel Ceiling, Vatican)

---

[5] Thomas Merton, *Dialogues with Silence: Prayers & Drawings*, ed. Jonathan Montaldo (San Francisco: HarperSanFranciso, 2001) 117.

The painting portrays Adam as being inanimate and waiting on the hand of God to invigorate his body with life. Robert Cumming observes, "Adam…seems to receive from God's right finger a charge which is beginning to run through his body like electricity giving him physical and spiritual life."[6] Of significance too is the left hand of God that touches the infant with the two fingers used to receive the Holy Communion. This gesture of sacramental touching conveys the promise of the Incarnate Word, which is the means by which life comes to humankind (John 3:16).[7] Listening for this incarnation that passes through the sacred space of existence is necessary if our lives are to be opened to the presence and nearness of God. Notice too the vague masks overlooking God's left hand just above the face of the infant. These have been interpreted as Lucifer and one of his followers.[8] These shadowy figures convey the ever-looming presence of all that is secondary or penultimate in life, which lures us into thinking we must possess in order to be whole always confusing the reality that wholeness only comes when we are possessed by God.

But how do we arrive at a point where we can experience the absolute silence necessary to hear God? How do we break ourselves of our selfishness that becomes intrusive on the divine presence? We must be intentional both with the call of faith and with the discipline of solitude that allows us to receive God's incarnation of love. What follows is something of a methodology suggesting how we might listen for the Divine. Listening is no exact science and the methods employed are myriad. But the task does require the need to center the soul and quiet the ego. Equally, there is need to focus

---

[6] Robert Cumming, *Art: The World's Greatest Paintings Explored and Explained* (London: A DK Publishing Book, 1995) 31.

[7] For a thorough analysis of the *Creation of Adam*, see William M. Jensen, "Who's Missing from Steinberg's 'Who's Who in Michelangelo's *Creation of Adam*,'" in *Interpreting Christian Art: Reflections on Christian Art*, eds. Heidi J. Hornik and Mikeal C. Parsons (Macon: Mercer University Press, 2004) 107–137.

[8] Ibid., 109.

on God, which the art of journaling can foster, and there is need to relate intentionally to the community of faith.

## Centering on Meaning

If each of us is to listen to God, there is need to center on life's meaning or purpose. Within the depth of our being is a yearning to make a difference through contributing to the good of the world. But too many of us get lost in the quest for making profit and pursuing a career. Others are consumed with the never-ending search for the pleasures of materialism and its insatiable demand that we buy more and more. In the process, the yearning to fulfill the deepest needs of our soul gets lost, and the ensuing confusion makes it difficult to hear God. If we are to listen, we must find a place of solitude and sacred space so that silence can become the objective of our meditation, which is necessary to discern God's call of love.

While it may seem odd to suggest that Christians consider the value of another religious perspective as a basis for centering on meaning, the Buddhists have much to offer those of us who comprise the Christian faith. The Buddhist tradition can remind those committed to Jesus Christ that there is a vital connection between the nurture of the inner life and the outward disposition and values. Central to the Buddhist way of thinking is that each of us has cravings and insatiable desires for things we think we need, but that lead only to misery in life. Think about how so many of us define who we are by where we live, our level of income, our titles, the kinds of clothes we wear, and automobiles we drive. According to the Buddhist teachings, these cravings lead to a sense of unhappiness in life because there is no ultimate satisfaction that can quench human desire. The way to overcome the unhappiness is to cease the cravings and the way to cease the cravings is through an eightfold path that leads to Enlightenment. This eightfold path consists of developing a reality that:

(1) maintains an awareness and knowledge of the cravings that lead to sadness;

(2) keeps emotions in balance;

(3) transforms speech in light of what we envision our world and future to be;

(4) engages in action borne out of kindness and generosity toward other living beings;

(5) seeks an occupation that contributes to life rather than taking from it;

(6) maintains a commitment to the effort and discipline required not to give in to cravings;

(7) commits to an intentional effort to concentrate and to empty the mind of all of the competitive energies that seek to control; and

(8) meditates in silence setting aside time for undistracted self-analysis in order to be fully aware of the direction and purpose for life.

The first two components relate to our understanding of life and focus on the degree of wisdom, insight, and understanding that direct our thinking. The next three, which are speech, action, and occupation, refer to our actions and conduct in the world. The last three address the meditative components that are required in order to concentrate on receiving peace. What results is a system that integrates our understanding, actions, and underlying emotional state.[9] Moreover, the system provides a way to concentrate on silence in order to enhance the possibilities of being aware of life's meaning and direction. From the faith perspective of the Christian worldview, the meditation of silence leads to the quieting of the mind and the stillness of the heart that results in the satisfaction of the soul, which makes it possible to hear God.

While the events of the cross and resurrection are alone of eternal significance because they testify to the God who acts in time in order to transform it, the Buddhists are on to something that

---

[9] Rupert Gethin, *The Foundations of Buddhism* (New York: Oxford University Press, 1998) 81–82.

those of the Christian faith would do well to consider. To assume that a methodology void of Christ is void of truth is a position of spiritual arrogance. Likewise, if we believe truly that Jesus is the way that leads to eternal life, there is no need to be defensive about the Christian faith. If God is infinite mystery, all that we know about him is revealed in Jesus Christ, but even this revelation cannot be fully comprehended. The reality is that none of us has unlimited access to the fullness of God. Each of us receives understanding from our own finite perspective. The critical need to listen recognizes our limitations of time and ability and our reliance on others to assist us in the journey toward the fullness of God that knows no end. Because of these limitations, the perspective of other world religions can contribute to our own need to discover truth just as many believe that Jesus Christ can make complete the teachings of other world religions. Learning to listen to others whose views—religious, political, or ethical—may be different from our own is the beginning of learning to listen to God. Not listening to others assumes that their perspective does not count. Further, how can a Christian have any hope of being heard if there is no genuine willingness to listen to and consider the value of another religious point of view?[10]

---

[10] Merton's prayer in Asia underscores the urgent need to listen to others in the name of God.

O God, we are one with You. You have made us one with You. You have taught us that, if we are open to one another, You dwell in us. Help us to preserve the openness and to fight for it with all our hearts. Help us to realize that there can be no understanding where there is mutual rejection.

O God, in accepting one another wholeheartedly, fully, Completely, we accept You, and we thank You, and we adore You, and we love You with our being, because our being is in Your being, our spirit is rooted in Your Spirit.

Fill us then with love and let us be bound together with love as We go our diverse ways, united in this one Spirit which makes You present to the world, and which makes You witness to the ultimate reality that is love. Love has overcome. Love is victorious. Amen. (*Dialogues with Silence*, 179)

Buddhism reminds us of the basic human instinct, which is that we want. The wants lead to sadness that too often disrupts our thoughts, emotions, speech, and actions. Emptiness is the human condition because, according to scripture, what we want ultimately is to be God. In Christian terms, God's love is infinite and the Divine's grace knows no bounds. We empty ourselves through the act of repentance in order to fill ourselves with the love of God that alone can make life meaningful. Hearing God becomes the process of being made whole through the ongoing act of salvation that Christians refer to as sanctification. Sanctification is similar to the path toward Enlightenment, which is the journey toward completeness in God. The insight is that where Enlightenment is understood in a Christian context as the process of sanctification, the eightfold path can serve as a method that helps each of us hear the gift of grace made possible through faith and complete surrender to Jesus Christ. He alone can fulfill the deepest longings and quell the disquieted soul that, if not addressed, will lead to a disruption of knowledge, speech, emotions, thoughts, and action.

The notion of borrowing from one faith to complement the Christian discipline of meditation may seem strange at best and completely anathema at worst. By way of analogy, allow me to suggest another approach the Christian might consider regarding the viability of the Buddhist eightfold path of Enlightenment. When I was a young child, I looked forward to visiting my aunt in Mississippi. She could bake the best coconut pie in the world. I am sure that the ingredients she used were similar to any number of recipes for coconut pies. But her coconut pies were different because she mixed the ingredients in her own special way with an added measure of only that which she could give—her love! This unique love is what made her pies so special. Similarly, many of the ingredients in the eightfold path toward Buddhist Enlightenment are evident in the Bible. Repeatedly, we are cautioned about the negative consequences of letting our emotions, thoughts, and desire get out of control. Think of the ancient story cautioning Cain to control his anger in order to avoid the sin that was waiting to destroy (Gen 4:5–7). Think of the disaster that befell King David because he did not maintain right mind, right emotions, and right aspirations in his pursuit of Bathsheba (1 Sam 11). What is unique about the Christian faith is that God takes the same ingredients provided in the recipe of Enlightenment and adds the extra and essential measure of agape love. His love acts in time to transform all time. There is need for each of us to recognize the spiritual vitality of a pure heart and pure mind, which lead to pure thoughts, emotions, speech, and calling. By deepening the awareness of each of these elements of being, we strengthen the vision of who we can become. Likewise, the concept of Enlightenment is applicable for the Christian journey only because Christ alone is the way that leads to redemptive life.

And in the way that leads to life, there is need to become aware of a more profound dimension in which one can experience God. Listening deepens our relationship with God. In considering how adults make sense of their world, Sharon Parks differentiates between what she describes as various forms of knowing. These forms are listed as "authority bound/dualistic," "unqualified relativism," "commitment in relativism," and "convictional commitment."[11] When these forms of knowing are related to faith development, they provide profound insight about the transition necessary to sustain an evolving awareness and commitment to God that can occur through the discipline of holy listening.

According to Parks, the first form of knowing is authority bound/dualistic, and individuals operating at this level tend to place unexamined trust in external authorities. An external authority that holds the key to the door of meaning disseminates truth. Individuals tend to think in categories of right versus wrong, us and them, and truth versus untruth. The basis for thinking in this category is often unexamined. Little assessment or critical reflection is made concerning the information or the "authority" who provides it. Knowledge of the experience of God and divine purpose for life

---

[11] Sharon Daloz Parks, *Big Questions/Worthy Dreams: Mentoring Young Adults in Their Search for Meaning, Purpose and Faith* (San Francisco: Jossey-Bass, 2000) 54.

reside with the experts who dictate the terms of faith for the believer. Trusting a process that is open and uncertain and that is entirely between the individual and God is foreign to this way of thinking, as there is need for an outside authority to interpret and inform the way to go and what to believe.

Parks observes that this form of thinking can begin to break down when life experiences do not correspond with what was previously told about truth. Traumatic encounters, education, and career changes are examples of alterations in experience that may call into question previously assumed and unquestioned categories of meaning.[12] This explains why many pastors encourage students leaving for college to be leery of those who teach lest they be led astray. Raising questions and teaching students to think for themselves can undermine the ability of many pastors to dictate the dualistic view of right versus wrong. No doubt, one can hear God at the authority bound/dualistic level of knowing. God can work with whatever form of knowing is utilized to experience his love. But the more the individual is willing to ponder, participate, and search, the more aware one can become of the depth of meaning from which wisdom can be drawn and the personal context in which the Divine can be manifest.

When an individual can no longer accept the external authority's role as declarer of truth and when life experiences begin to confuse the simplicity of the absolutist approach, Parks maintains that some move on to a stage of "unqualified relativism." The individual comes to see that had they been reared in a different family or culture, their perceptions of authority and right versus wrong may have been viewed differently. They begin to remove the blinders that culture places on their way of observing, and their thinking about meaning starts to change. Long-held assumptions regarded as beliefs begin to be questioned and attitudes about meaning begin to be analyzed. Understood less and less in absolute terms, knowledge begins to be embraced as relative in nature and as

---

[12] Ibid., 55.

conditional upon life experiences. Truth in this way of thinking becomes relative to the individual possessing the truth.[13]

But, as Parks observes, "This position of unqualified relativism is difficult to sustain over time." [14] At some point, everyone needs a place to stand. The assumption that each individual can claim what is true inevitably leads many to ponder the difference between opinions and hopes that are, as Parks writes, "grounded in careful and thoughtful observation and reflection."[15] Life, afterall, itself has a way of bearing down upon us generating the need for some imperative of meaning and commitment.

The lack of certainty over time requires that one consider the next stage of meaning where there is "commitment in relativism."[16] This level provides the opportunity for transition to more profound meaning where responsibility for thinking and making meaning for oneself begins to occur. A commitment emerges in a sea of choices. No longer content to live as if anything goes, this person seeks a sense of direction and a mission by which to live. Also, life becomes viewed in the way that one observes a painting. The more the observer can move from one point to another, the more perspective one can ascertain about the nature of the painting. Construction of a place to stand is sought even as there is awareness that there are multiple positions from which to choose. Part of becoming an adult is the ability to say, "I will go down this road and not another."

The final form of knowing that Parks describes is that of "convictional commitment." This level comprises recognition of wisdom that is able to distinguish between everyday hopes and the kind of hope that sustains no matter what circumstances might arise. The individual gives way to the simplicity on the other side of complexity that recognizes the freedom borne out of dependency on grace. Truth in doctrine gives way to a journey of transformation that leaves open the possibility of coming to

---

[13] Ibid., 59.
[14] Ibid.
[15] Ibid.
[16] Ibid.

understand God in new and more meaningful ways in light of life's circumstances and experiences.[17] No longer is there need to defend one's faith or to judge those who hold differing views. There is only the desire to live in the goodness of God's love and to be sustained by divine hope regardless of the prevailing circumstances of the day.

Applying Parks's concept to a Christian priority for living, truth begins to be discerned not so much by the external authorities and their power to persuade but rather by spiritual priorities that quietly begin to emerge in stillness of the heart generating a desire for integrity, character, justice, mercy, kindness, humility, goodness, service, sacrifice, and love. The perpetual aimlessness of relativity gives way in time to a sense of convictions grounded in a Christian ethic of humility and love.

The critical questions articulated at the convictional commitment stage are not characterized in terms of right versus wrong. Some of the pivotal questions become:

(1) What does it mean to be Christian?
(2) How do we grow in faith?
(3) How do we avoid being dogmatic?
(4) How do we avoid being relativistic?
(5) How do we find home in the midst of the journey?

Questions like these distinguish between faith that operates in fixed, dualistic forms of knowing and faith that seeks to deepen and expand over the course of one's life. The convictional commitment stage seeks to grow toward a more profound dimension of God's love and seeks to connect awareness of this love with activity and presence in the world.

Moving toward the convictional commitment stage is important because of the depth of self-awareness that begins to emerge. Self-awareness is central to answering such questions because we are keenly aware at this stage of the struggle within our

---

[17] Ibid., 60.

own being to succumb to the chaos of the world or discover God anew in each moment that we live.

At issue is the age-old struggle between the soul and the ego. The soul is the essence of life from a biblical perspective and is understood as the life-force that is not at rest until we are living out our calling as the incarnation of love. The soul longs to please God and it longs to connect with others. The Bible does not understand each of as having a soul but rather sees each of us as a living, breathing soul. Our lives are owed to the Creator who feels us with the very breath of God. To live is to live for God by being the incarnation to each other. Physical life merely exists apart from this recognition and commitment. According to Eugene Peterson, Jesus put it this way, "Calling the crowd to join his disciples, he said, 'Anyone who intends to come with me has to let me lead. You're not in the driver's seat; I am. Don't run from suffering; embrace it. Follow me and I'll show you how. Self-help is no help at all. Self-sacrifice is the way, my way, to saving yourself, your true self. What good would it do to get everything you want and lose you, the real you? What could you ever trade your soul for?'" (Mark 8:34–37, The Message).[18]

Conversely, the ego longs to please self and is a powerful force that directs our wants allowing them to be confused with our needs. The ego lifts the self as the center of all that is. Unconsciously, the ego drives to establish our priorities based upon selfish interests. Even in matters of religion, the ego can be a destructive force. Too often, power and the ability to control become the infectious arms of the ego. Winning at the expense of an ethic of agape love is the false spirit of the ego. Paul himself expressed this tension within each of us when he wrote, "I do not understand my own actions. For I do not do what I want, but I do the very thing I hate" (Rom 7:15, NRSV). Paul's remedy was the cross, which shatters the ego's

---

bent toward selfishness and allows the soul to turn toward trust in God.[19]

The tension between the soul and the ego can be destructive if it is not addressed. The need to listen is of profound importance because listening requires that one move beyond the selfish demands of the ego to an awareness of the longing of the soul to connect with others and with God. Jesus said, "For where your treasure is, there your heart will be also" (Matt 6:21, NRSV). The only treasure that really mattered to Jesus was the heart of love fueled by the grace of the Divine, as understood in his commandment that we love each other even as he loves us (John 15:12). When the soul can be driven by agape love, the ability to hear God's purpose is realized.

But to hear God requires silence, which leads one to confession. Confession opens one to calling. Calling connects each person in the community of faith and the community of faith in turn realizes opportunities to be incarnate love in the world in which we live. But communities of faith need to provide a context in which people can explore their faith with integrity free from repression. Sadly, too many churches provide too little time for a growing awareness of what it means to be called into the world. In my own Baptist tradition, we have become experts at "teaching" the faith at the expense of trusting individuals with opportunities to explore faith in ways that lead to a deeper, personal experience and awareness of God. James Fowler notes:

> Something on the order of 90 percent of our interviews with adults ended with the respondent—following two and a half hours of intense conversation—saying something like this: "I really appreciate this experience; I *never* (sic.) get an opportunity to talk about these things...." From this experience, I have come to believe

---

[19] See Paul Fiddes' discussion on the ego in *Past Event and Present Salvation: The Christian Idea of Atonement* (Louisville: Westminster/John Knox Press, 1989) 147–50.

that it is most important to provide occasions for people to express in words, in action, in contemplation, "the faith that is in them."[20]

How can we find a structure where we can voice in contemplation, words, and actions who God is calling us to be? Is there a way in which we can embrace all that Christ yearns for us to realize about his love and his expectation to be that love in the world? Journaling is one source of contemplation that requires intentional reflection through reading scripture, through assessing our individual wants and priorities in light of calling, and through recognition of our own spiritual autobiography, which is the story of God's grace in the lives of those whose own faith has forever expanded our horizon of divine love.

## Intentional Journaling

Intentional journaling is a meditative experience that entails a written record of thoughts, ideas, and emotions that result from reading scripture, assessing personal priorities, and from reflection on a spiritual biography. Prior to engaging in any of these tasks, it will be helpful to find a quiet place to relax in order to encounter the stillness from which to start the journaling process.[21] Begin by relaxing the muscles in the legs, stomach, arms, and throat. As you breathe, pay attention to the rising and the falling of the abdominal muscles. Listen for the light within. And begin to experience the presence of God that is all around us but so seldom felt. In addition to the journal, meditation can help relax and foster attentiveness to the inner self even as we go from one task to the next or from one office to the next in the course of the daily grind. Even as we walk, we can ponder the process of each breath that represents the life of God within us. By doing so, we prepare our hearts and minds for the more intensive journaling experience.

---

[20] James W. Fowler, "Faith and the Structure of Meaning" in *Faith Development and Fowler*, ed. Craig Dykstra and Sharon Parks (Birmingham AL: Religious Education Press, 1986) 38.

[21] See Richard Peace, *Spiritual Journaling: Recording Your Journey toward God* (Colorado Springs CO: NavPress, 1998).

*Reading Scripture.* A part of journaling is the intentional reflection on scripture. Begin in prayer. Then read the selected biblical passage not so much from the standpoint of confirming what is already known or for justifying what you want to do, but rather from the perspective of gaining new insight and deeper awareness of God's presence. Too often, scripture is read in order to memorize material to prove a theological point and support a particular agenda. But of need is to read the Bible in ways that allow God's Spirit to convict instead of merely to confirm. One way to read the Bible authentically and to minimize biases or preconceptions is to read it from the perspective of the different characters that are a part of the biblical drama. For example, too often the tendency is to look judgmentally upon those who do not recognize Jesus as the living Christ. But what are ways in which Christians can be like Pharisees? Remember James and John, who were the sons of Zebedee? They came to Jesus and he asked them, "What do you want me to do for you?" They responded by asking him to grant their wish that they be allowed to sit on his right and left hands in glory. They did not get it. Why? Are they alone, or perhaps we often miss the point as well. The point that James and John missed is further highlighted when Jesus asked the same question to Blind Bartimaeus. Jesus asked again, "What do you want me to do for you?" to which there was the simple faith response, "Let me see again" (Mark 10:35–52, NRSV).

Similarly, Jesus is asking each of us every time we seek his presence, "What do you want me to do for you?" The discerning listener is far more preoccupied with hearing and seeing anew God's love than about sitting on the left or right hand in glory. Interacting with scripture in this way can lead to a conversation with God that is fundamentally preoccupied not so much with the need to tell God what we want, but just with the simple need to listen to the images and ideas of love that begin to emerge as we sit in silence. As reading the Bible in this way began in prayer, so too the reflective study of the biblical passage should end in prayer. Then write about the biblical narrative as it was experienced in reading the drama by placing yourself in alternative roles. Note the new insights and feelings that occur. Contemplate the new understanding and dictate what new actions or commitments need to be made.

*Evaluating Priorities.* Another way to journal is to reflect on our mission or calling. Listening to the soul requires an acknowledgment that there are consequences to our wants. The outcome for which we hope drives what we do. Means matter. Consequently, our wants need to be measured in terms of priorities, mission, and life's purpose. Financial planners often remind us that the financial decisions made today impact the quality of life for tomorrow's retirement. Emphasis is placed on planning and a premium is made on wise investments that bring about maximum opportunities. Knowing what is wanted and what is important become paramount as a "financial road" is envisioned for how each of us gets where we hope to be. Such a perspective for calling, faith development, and spirituality is much more necessary and carries with it much more profound implications for the future of this life and the eternity to come. The following diagram can be of help in discerning God's priorities for living, as it allows opportunity to assess what is important in life as well as to consider the consequences for decisions and actions that are made.

## Assessing Calling

What do I have that gives me joy?

Why do these people, things, etc. give me joy?

What do I currently want that I think will give me more joy and satisfaction?

What are the consequences if I get what I want?
    To self?

    To others?

For what do I want to be remembered? What is my calling or purpose in life?

How are my wants and priorities adjusted when viewed in light of my purpose and calling?

Each individual should begin the exercise by examining what currently gives life meaning. What is it that provides sustaining joy? What things bring satisfaction? What kinds of task are enjoyed? Who are the people with whom you share your life? Second, ask yourself, "Why do these things, tasks, and/or people give me joy?" This point in the exercise can open us to an awareness of how easily each of us becomes consumed with things and career at the expense of people. Reminding ourselves of the love of family and friends is a part of also being open to the love of God. Third, think about things that you find yourself currently wishing you had. What do you find yourself wanting that you unconsciously tell yourself you need in order to feel accepted, happy, or whole? What's going on? Why is it that you feel you need these particular items and/or people at this point in your life? How will gaining these contribute to your life? What difference will they make in your life or in the lives of others? Is the task, item, or person necessary in order to fill your life with God's love? This is an important dimension of the exercise because our world is bombarded with messages from tomato soup to automobiles that are trying to convince us to purchase just the product we need in order to be fulfilled. Being able to distinguish between what we need in order to be God's love and what we want because somebody has promised us that the item is a tonic that can make us happy or give us pleasure is crucial in the art of listening to God. One sure way to get at this distinction is to move to the fourth step in the reflective process, which is to examine the consequences of our wants for our lives as well as the lives of others who will be impacted by our actions and decisions. Once you have thought about what you are currently wanting and what its impact might be on others, move to the fifth component of the assignment, which is to examine how you want to be remembered. What is life's ultimate purpose? Many people think about immediate actions with little regard for how it will impact their life or what the long-term consequences might be. But crucial in faith discernment is the need to think about life from destiny's end. When our days are done, will we have contributed to God's kingdom of love or to our own selfish pursuits? What is the great cathedral we are building stone by stone that will be a legacy to those who follow? Thinking in this way reminds us of the spiritual road we are called to follow. Just like financial planning, the path we choose results in the destiny to which we arrive. Once you have thought about how you want to invest in the future of your life, address the final component, which is to see if your wants and priorities have changed. If so, list the adjusted wants and priorities and claim them as the benchmarks toward which to move even as God is trusted each step of the way.

*Spiritual Autobiography.* Being required to put one's life experience in print is not something most of us take time to do, yet many forgotten people and experiences accompany our journey. They have shaped us for good and for bad. If you doubt this, consider writing your own spiritual autobiography. List those people, times, places, and events where you have been changed. Think of those people who bought stock in you as you were because they saw what you would become. Think too about the impact of choices at those critical junctures in life that resulted in a transformation of the soul. I like to speak not so much of a salvation experience, but rather of salvation experiences. The comment often is received with a look of puzzlement. Yet there are pivotal points in my life where I have come to understand God, myself, and others in new ways that have made faith more meaningful and real. These pivotal moments have not "saved me" in the traditional sense, but they have opened me to a deeper awareness of the presence of God in my life and my need to be this presence in the lives of others.

For example, Sarah Granade was my seventh grade Sunday school teacher. She and many of those who worked in the youth program at church impressed upon me at an early age that it was permissible to be a Christian and to think. They helped me to see that I did not have to divorce my mind from my heart. Even more importantly, they modeled faith for me and helped me to link the piety of Sunday with the ethics of the rest of the week. Conversely, with chronic ear problems, I was quite sick as a child and often missed school. The result was that I was placed in a slower reading group. I remember the taunts of the children in the accelerated program and, to this day, that experience has made me sensitive to those who hurt and, for whatever reason, are not able to move at as rapid a pace as others. Many others also blessed my life by helping mold me, and they remain the grace of God for having done so. My point is that all of us would do well to take some time and write in our journal the significant events and people that have shaped our lives. You say, "I can't do this." But start writing. You will be amazed at the people and stories that just flow from your soul to the page. These people and experiences are the pages of the book that make up the narrative of your life. People who have been the grace and voice of incarnation have helped you listen to the Divine. Experiences have molded you. For good or bad, you carry the lessons learned, albeit unconsciously, every step of the way. Journaling your autobiography is important because, as Richard Peace observes, "Growth involves dealing with the past so that you move beyond it into wholeness."[22] In emphasizing the importance of spiritual autobiography, Peace encourages individuals to list in their journals significant persons who are living or deceased and who are nearby or distant; to record injuries and illnesses as well as physical activities; and to record events, both personal and societal, that for good or bad have had and important impact on our lives.[23] By doing so, an awareness of the ongoing creation and calling within each of us will begin to emerge.

## Intentional Community

There is need within the church to foster communities that allow persons the freedom to discuss their own journeys. So much of listening to God can be enhanced through the opportunity provided when individuals can live and be accepted in a community where they are free to share their limitations as well as their hopes.

Creating small group opportunities where people have a context in which to reflect on their faith and calling and to discuss opportunities of service will be critical for the future of the church

---

[22] Ibid., 44.
[23] Ibid., 46–47.

in the postmodern world. Western culture is undergoing the most radical shift since the Reformation. Too many churches still cling to a modern framework that assumes there is one single truth to which the majority of citizens subscribe. Throughout much of the twentieth century, the church was able to flourish in the United States because it reveled as the main show. The church provided a spiritual umbrella where most Americans pursued truth. In the postmodern world in which we now live, truth has become relative. This is not to say that the Christian truth is less relevant. But the authority with which the church once spoke is no longer as uniform and, therefore, as dominant. There are too many options available, and the understanding of truth dispensed from a once central authority no longer exists. Christianity is now required to communicate in a world of competing ideas. In such a world, the church is being required—if not intentionally, most certainly out of a need to survive—to work with and relate to alternative and diverse positions. The good news in such a world of transition is that the church has an opportunity to rediscover its call to have an impassioned love for the stranger that rests at the heart of the Gospel.

The challenge for the church is to develop alternative forms of worship focused on fostering spiritual transformation. For example, the traditional model of the institutional church that insists upon heavy division between the authoritative clergy and the passive and governed laity is no longer viable for many seeking spiritual guidance. Equally true is the need to realize that a triumphal demeanor and a disposition of spiritual arrogance will not be sufficient. What will be of utmost necessity is the need to live in such a way that people see and are drawn to the experience of Jesus Christ through the willingness of the believer to be the incarnation of love. Far more important than defending doctrine is the need of people to embrace their call as the heart, head, hands, and ears of Jesus. Words attributed to St. Francis of Assisi are worth noting. He reportedly said, "Preach the word of God wherever you go, even use words, if necessary." More than a defender of the faith, the relevancy of the church in the postmodern world will be measured by the degree to which the church understands itself as the vehicle of incarnational experience whereby others are drawn into the community through a relationship of love.

Creating an intentional environment within the church where people can explore the spirituality of listening is paramount. Parker Palmer's observation about teaching is applicable to spiritual development in the postmodern world. He writes, "In the Christian tradition, truth is not a concept that 'works' but an incarnation that lives.... Education of this sort means more than teaching the facts and learning the reasons so we can manipulate life toward our ends. It means being drawn into a personal responsiveness and accountability to each other and the world of which we are a part."[24] But how can such a church be framed? Is it entirely necessary to have Sunday morning worship? Must this worship always be centered around a service where the pastor delivers the message to people in pews where all look to the sacred pulpit? Such worship is important, but it can no longer be expected to serve as the only model. Perhaps additional forms of worship can begin to be framed around the creation of small group communities that consist of about ten to twelve people.[25] In such a context, people come together in informal settings in order to discuss spiritual ideas with their pastor and each other and people intentionally seek diversity of perspective in order to enhance the dialogue. Central to the formation of such groups is the realization that each one of us sees through a dim mirror and that no one of us has the right to judge the commitment and integrity of another. For such groups to serve as contexts in which authentic, honest, and free faith can emerge, participants will need to recognize that far more necessary than being right or wrong on any particular doctrinal or ethical issue is

---

[24] Parker J. Palmer, *To Know as We are Known: Education as a Spiritual Journey* (San Francisco: HarperSanFrancisco, 1993) 14–15.

[25] See W. Brendan Reddy, *Intervention Skills: Process Consultation for Small Groups and Teams* (San Francisco: Jossey-Bass, 1994) 9. Reddy maintains that small groups cease to be small when they exceed a group size of twelve members.

the need to be God's love in a world that is thirsty for the incarnation's gift of redemption.

Focusing on young adults between the ages of seventeen and thirty, Parks provides an important insight for the future of the church concerning how each of us needs to take responsibility for framing our worldview. Parks observes that the young adult age group is the time when "a distinctive mode of meaning-making can emerge" that includes "becoming critically aware of one's own composing of reality, self-consciously participating in an ongoing dialogue toward truth and cultivating a capacity to respond—to act—in ways that are satisfying and just."[26] There is equal need to provide opportunity for all in the church to move beyond authoritarian concepts of worship where adherents receive information passively to a context where each individual has the opportunity (and responsibility) to dialogue, reflect, and act on the relevancy of the Christian truth for his or her world and calling.

A group of men who helped me move taught me a valuable lesson about community. As I listened to the men, I observed that everybody was referred to as "boss." I was "boss." John was "boss." Tom was "boss." Everybody did what he had to do to help each other get the job done. Each person was the boss to everybody else. In the course of the day, these men helped me do something I could not have done by myself, and they helped each other. Among them, there was no hierarchy and no division of classes. All were equal and all were equally committed to getting the task done. I could not help but think this is what being church ought to be like! Intentional communities where all are equal in their call to serve and all are committed to the work of incarnational love will be critical for the future of the church in the postmodern world where new patterns of meaning are constantly emerging.

---

[26] Parks, *Big Questions/Worthy Dreams*, 5–6.

My colleague, Rob Nash, and I spent thirteen weeks working in such an intentional community.[27] Laypeople volunteered to work with us over a thirteen-week period to discuss three questions: (1) who is Jesus? (2) what is the church? and (3) who is Jesus in this church? We emphasized the need for laypersons .to take responsibility for their spiritual formation, to be opened to their calling, and to understand that the extent to which each of us sees God as love is the extent to which we will be that love in the world. We encouraged a transformation of lay participation in church life that is based upon the concept of the local church as a mission outpost and upon the idea that the Christian calling extends to every facet of life. We suggested that the church begin to think beyond itself as an institution of brick and mortar. Participants were asked to contemplate ways they might extend the institution itself into the various communities where they lived and worked. After weeks of discussion and reflection, one member of the group confessed:

> I have lived in the same neighborhood for almost thirty years. Over time, I have seen so many of my friends leave. Their children and our children have grown up and moved away. Some of my neighbors have moved on to other communities. Some have died. And in the transition, new people have come. But they are not like me. They do not go to church. I can't tell you how many times I have driven by and thought to myself, "It is sad that no one takes them to church." In this group, we keep being asked to think about being the hands and heart of Jesus. We are told that our world has changed. We are reminded that maybe it's time to think about doing church differently. Well, I think it's time for me to quit lamenting that so many children in my neighborhood don't go to church, and it's time for me to bring church to my neighborhood!

This participant got it. The intentional community changed her life because it empowered her to be a minister in her world. She

---

[27] Rob N. Nash and Robert Shippey, "EMBRACE: Experiencing More by Realizing All Christ Expects," Fifth Avenue Baptist Church, Rome GA, September–November, 2003.

listened to the divine Spirit stirring within her soul. She concluded that she would begin a lay Bible study initiative in the neighborhood. By doing so, she embraced her call to extend the walls of worship by being the church in an environment where many by circumstance or choice were unchurched. She claimed her role as a priest in a mission outpost in the name of God!

*Beginnings*

The Chinese have a proverb that says, "We climb the mountain one step at a time." In developing the discipline of holy listening, climbing the mountain one step at a time is imperative. Sometimes there may be need to step back, pause, and then resume the climb. Much patience, humor, forgiveness, and grace is necessary. Listening in a loud world is difficult. It is easy to give up and even easier never to start. There are so many who already have the answers and are more than willing to impart their special knowledge. But genuine listening of the heart borne out of complete devotion to God requires intentional effort in a loud world.

In reflecting on the value of Quaker worship, Douglas Steere acknowledges that unless there is the realization of the countless distractions that can disrupt the art of listening, silence can "disintegrate...into a boring state of deadness [and] into a situation of vegetative stagnation."[28] Fear of such is perhaps why so many are reluctant to engage in silence. I remember discussing the importance of silence and its inclusion in worship with a group of pastors. I am sure there was an excitement in my voice as I encouraged the group to utilize silence as a part of worship. After the meeting, one of the pastors pulled me aside. He was polite and gracious, but said, "You need to realize that our people won't stand for silence!" I should not have been surprised. Our age is one of constant messaging, and the demand is for entertainment and

---

[28] Douglas V. Steere, "On Listening to Another," in *The Doubleday Devotional Classics*, ed. E. Glenn Hinson (New York: Doubleday & Company, Inc., 1978) 3:229.

activity, even in worship. Being aware of the distractions that can assuage our awareness of God is paramount. But in all our efforts to create meaningful worship, where is the silence that opens each one of us to the deep presence of God? What does the Divine want us to hear? How do the noisy gongs and clanging cymbals (1 Cor 13:1) of our worship offered to please God in fact silence the love with which the Divine desires to stir our being? Was the pastor correct? Is there no one left who will stand for silence in worship? Perhaps some yet are willing to embrace silence and recognize its hallowed entry as the place for listening to the still small voice of God.

I do believe that beyond all activity and beyond all words is the silence of the Holy who forever seeks to stir the light of love from within. John Woolman spoke of how an inward reliance on God and an accompanying humility opened him to this divine love and led him to pray "that no secret reserve in my heart might hinder my access to the divine fountain."[29] The experience of the silence remains the spring from which the divine fountain of love flows and is the source from which each of us is called in the home and the world and at work as well as worship. Those who have ears, eyes, hearts, and minds to listen may just hear the subtle sound of love, which is nonetheless real.

---

[29] John Woolman, "The Journal of John Woolman," in *The Doubleday Devotional Classics*, ed. E. Glenn Hinson (New York: Doubleday & Company, Inc., 1978) 2:287.

# Bibliography

Achtemeier, Paul J. *The Inspiration of Scripture: Problems and Proposals*. Philadelphia: The Westminster Press, 1980.

Adler, Ronald B., Lawrence B. Rosenfeld, and Neil Towne. *Interplay: The Process of Interpersonal Communication*. Fort Worth: Harcourt Brace College Publishers, 1995.

Aleshire, Daniel O. *Faith Care: Ministering to All God's People through the Ages of Life*. Philadelphia: The Westminster Press, 1988.

Augustine. *The Confessions of St. Augustine*. Translated by John K. Ryan. New York: Image Books, 1960.

Barth, Karl. *Church Dogmatics*. Edited by G. W. Bromiley and T. F. Torrance. 13 volumes. Edinburgh: T. & T. Clark, 1932–1969.

———. *Wolfgang Amadeus Mozart*. Translated by Clarence K. Pott. Grand Rapids: William B. Eerdmans Publishing Company, 1986.

Berry, Wendell. *A Timbered Choir: The Sabbath Poems 1979–1997*. Washington, DC: Counterpoint, 1998.

Claypool, John. "Samuel: Crossing Where It's Narrow." *Glad Reunion: Meeting Ourselves in the Lives of Bible Men and Women*. Waco: Word Incorporated, 1985.

*Contemporary English Version*. New York: American Bible Society, 1995.

Cumming, Robert. *Art: The World's Greatest Paintings Explored and Explained*. London: ADK Publishing Book, 1995.

Daloz, Laurent A. *Mentor: Guiding the Journey of Adult Learners*. San Francisco: Jossey-Bass Publishers, 1999.

deSilva, David A. *Honor, Patronage, Kinship & Purity: Unlocking New Testament Culture*. Downers Grove IL: InterVarsity Press, 2000.

Duling, Dennis C. "Interpreting the New Testament." In *The New Testament: History, Literature, and Social Context*. 4th edition. New York: Wadsworth, 2003.

Eliot, T. S. "The Four Quartets." In *The Complete Poems and Plays:
1909–1950*. New York: Harcourt, Brace and World, Inc, 1971.
———. "The Wasteland." *The Norton Anthology of Poetry*. Edited by
Alexander W. Allison, et al. 3rd edition. New York: W. W. Norton
& Company, 1983.

Fiddes, Paul. *Past Event and Present Salvation: The Christian Idea of
Atonement* Louisville KY: Westminster/John Knox Press, 1989.

Fowler, James W. "Faith and the Structure of Meaning." In *Faith
Development and Fowler*. Edited by Craig Dykstra and Sharon Parks.
Birmingham AL: Religious Education Press, 1986.

Foster, Richard J. *Celebration of Discipline: The Path to Spiritual Growth*.
San Francisco: Harper San Francisio, 1988.

Garrett, James Leo. *Systematic Theology: Biblical, Historical & Evangelical*.
Volume 1. Grand Rapids: William B. Eerdmans Publishing
Company, 1990.

Gethin, Rupert. *The Foundations of Buddhism*. New York: Oxford
University Press, 1998.

Hull, William E. *The Christian Experience of Salvation: Layman's Library of
Christian Doctrine*. Nashville: Broadman Press, 1987.

Isaacson, Walter. "Citizen Ben's Seven Great Virtues." *Time* 102/1 (7
July 2003): 40–53.

Jensen, William M. "Who's Missing from Steinberg's 'Who's Who in
Michelangelo's *Creation of Adam*.'" In *Interpreting Christian Art:
Reflections on Christian Art*. Edited by Heidi J. Hornik and Mikeal C.
Parsons. Macon GA: Mercer University Press, 2004.

John of the Cross. *Dark Night of the Soul: A Classic in the Literature of
Mysticism*. Translated and edited by E. Allison Peers. Garden City
NY: Image Books, 1959.

Johnson, L. D. *The Morning after Death*. Nashville: Broadman Press,
1978.

Johnson, William G. *Hebrews: Knox Preaching Guides*. Edited by John H.
Hayes. Atlanta: John Knox Press, 1980.

Jones, Peter Rhea. "Preaching from Romans." *Review and Expositor* 3/4
(Fall 1976): 474.

Kraus, Hans-Joachim. *Theology of the Psalms*. Translated by Keith Crim.
Minneapolis: Augsburg Publishing House, 1986.

Lewis, C. S. *The Problem of Pain*. New York: Macmillan Publishing Company, 1962.

——. *The Screwtape Letters*. New York: MacMillan Publishing Company, 1961.

Merton, Thomas. *Dialogues with Silence: Prayers and Drawings*. Edited by Jonathan Montaldo. San Francisco: Harper San Francisco, 2001.

Moltmann, Jürgen. *Theology of Hope*. Translated by James W. Leitch. London: SCM Press, 1967.

Moody, Dale. *The Word of Truth: A Summary of Christian Doctrine Based on Biblical Revelation*. Grand Rapids: William B. Eerdmans Publishing Company, 1981.

Nash, Rob N., and Robert Shippey. "EMBRACE: Experiencing More by Realizing All Christ Expects." Fifth Avenue Baptist Church. Rome, Georgia, September–November, 2003.

*New International Version*. Nashville: Broadman & Homan Publishers, 1986.

*New American Standard Bible*. La Habra CA: The Lockman Foundation, 1995.

*New Living Translation*. Carol Stream IL: Tyndale House Publishers, Inc., 2003.

*New Revised Standard Version*. New York: Oxford University Press, 1991.

Nouwen, Henri J. M. *The Return of the Prodigal Son: A Story of Homecoming*. New York: Image Books, 1994.

Palmer, Parker J. *Let Your Life Speak: Listening for the Voice of Vocation*. San Francisco: Jossey-Bass, 2000.

——. *To Know as We Are Known: Education as a Spiritual Journey*. San Francisco: HarperSanFrancisco, 1993.

Parks, Sharon Daloz. *Big Questions/Worthy Dreams: Mentoring Young Adults in Their Search for Meaning, Purpose and Faith*. San Francisco: Jossey-Bass, 2000.

Peace, Richard. *Spiritual Journaling: Recording Your Journey toward God*. Colorado Springs CO: NavPress, 1998.

Phillips, J. B. *Your God Is Too Small*. New York: Touchstone by Simon & Schuster, 1997.

Raines, Robert. *Creative Broodings*. New York: Macmillan Publishing Company, 1966.

Rilke, Rainer Maria. *Letters to a Young Poet*. Translated by M. D. Herter Norton. New York: Norton, 1993.

Reddy, W. Brendan. *Intervention Skills: Process Consultation for Small Groups and Teams*. San Francisco: Jossey-Bass, 1994.

Robinson, John A. T. *The Human Face of God*. Philadelphia: The Westminster Press, 1973.

Schillebeeckx, Edward. *Jesus: An Experiment in Christology*. New York: Crossroad, 1981.

Shippey, Margaret. "Living with Juvenile Diabetes." Cleveland Kiwanis Club, Cleveland GA, Spring 2001.

Simon, Paul. *Best of Simon and Garfunkel*. Sony, 1999.

Steere, Douglas V. "On Listening to Another." In *The Doubleday Devotional Classics*. Edited by E. Glenn Hinson. Volume 3. New York: Doubleday & Company, Inc., 1978.

Stroup, George W. *The Promise of Narrative Theology: Recovering the Gospel in the Church*. Atlanta: John Knox Press, 1981.

*The Living New Testament: Paraphrased*. Wheaton: Tyndale House Foundation, 1967.

*The Message*. Colorado Springs CO: NavPress Publishing Group. 1993, 1994, 1995, 1996, 2000, 2001, 2002.

Thompson, William M. *The Jesus Debate: A Survey & Synthesis*. New York: Paulist Press, 1985.

Tillich, Paul. *Christianity and the Existentialists*. Edited by Carl Michalson. New York: Charles Scribner's Sons, 1956.

———. *The Courage to Be*. New Haven: Yale University Press, 1952.

———. *Dynamics of Faith*. New York: Harper Torchbooks, 1957.

———. *Systematic Theology: Three Volumes in One*. Chicago: The University of Chicago Press, 1967.

———. "The Right Time." *The New Being*. New York: Charles Scribner's Sons, 1955.

———. "The Yoke of Religion." *The Shaking of the Foundations*. New York: Charles Scribner's Sons, 1976.

Tupper, E. Frank. *A Scandalous Providence: The Jesus Story of the Compassion of God*. Macon GA: Mercer University Press, 1995.

———. "Lectures on Fallenness." Lectures, The Southern Baptist Theological Seminary, Louisville KY, spring semester, 1987.

von Rad, Gerhard. *Genesis: A Commentary*. Philadelphia: The Westminster Press, 1972.

Wallis, Jim. "Where do Enron Executives go to Church?" *SojoNet 2001*, 17 January 2002 <*http://www.sojonet*>.

Weiser, Artur. *The Psalms: A Commentary*. Philadelphia: The Westminster Press, 1962.

Woolman, John. "The Journal of John Woolman." In *The Doubleday Devotional Classics*. Edited by E. Glenn Hinson. Volume 2. New York: Doubleday & Company, Inc., 1978.

Wright, N. T. *The Challenge of Jesus: Rediscovering Who Jesus Was and Is*. Downers Grove: Intervarsity Press, 1999.

Wooten, Sid. E-mail message to author. 14 August 2003.

Younger, Brett. "Thanking God for Broadway Baptist Church." Broadway Baptist Church. Fort Worth TX. 20 July 2003. Church Newsletter.

Younger, Carol. "Swimming with the Prophets." *Prophetic Ethics: Christian Reflection* (Winter 2003): 70.

# Index

CPSIA information can be obtained at www.ICGtesting.com
Printed in the USA
LVOW081101271212

313378LV00001B/105/A